TOSEL®

JUNIOR

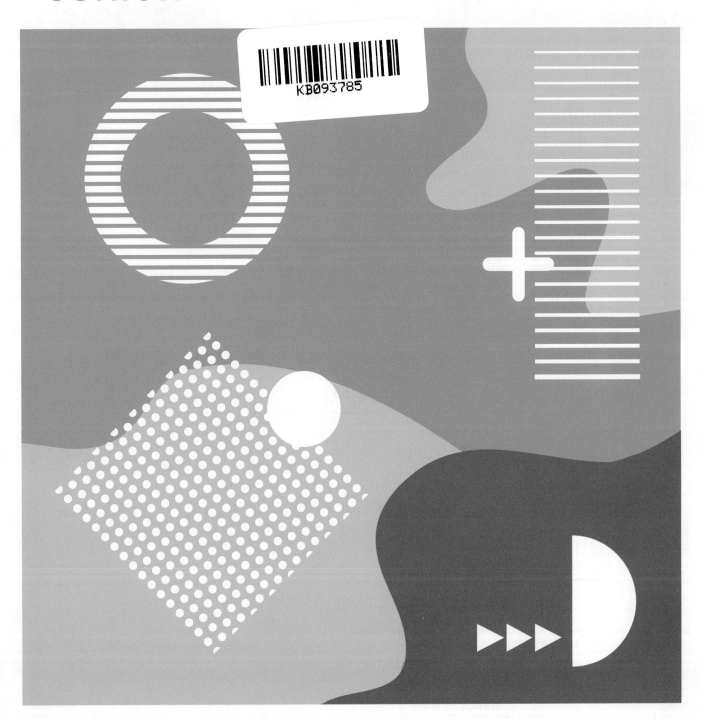

International
TOSEL
Committee

GRAMMAR 2

CONTENTS

TOSEL® Level Chart
TOSEL 단계표

COCOON

아이들이 접할 수 있는 공식 인증 시험의 첫 단계로써, 아이들의 부담을 줄이고 즐겁게 흥미를 유발할 수 있도록 컬러풀한 색상과 디자인으로 시험지를 구성하였습니다.

Pre-STARTER

친숙한 주제에 대한 단어, 짧은 대화, 짧은 문장을 사용한 기본적인 문장표현 능력을 측정합니다.

STARTER

흔히 접할 수 있는 주제와 상황과 관련된 주제에 대한 짧은 대화 및 짧은 문장을 이해하고 일상생활 대화에 참여하며 실질적인 영어 기초 의사소통 능력을 측정합니다.

BASIC

개인 정보와 일상 활동, 미래 계획, 과거의 경험에 대해 구어와 문어의 형태로 의사소통을 할 수 있는 능력을 측정합니다.

JUNIOR

일반적인 주제와 상황을 다루는 회화와 짧은 단락, 실용문, 짧은 연설 등을 이해하고 간단한 일상 대화에 참여하는 능력을 측정합니다.

HIGH JUNIOR

넓은 범위의 사회적, 학문적 주제에서 영어를 유창하고 정확하게, 효과적으로 사용할 수 있는 능력 및 중문과 복잡한 문장을 포함한 다양한 문장구조의 사용 능력을 측정합니다.

ADVANCED

대학 및 대학원에서 요구되는 영어능력과 취업 또는 직업근무환경에 필요한 실용영어 능력을 측정합니다.

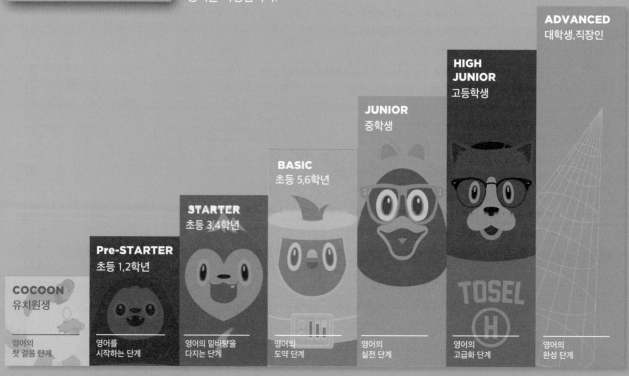

COCOON
유치원생
영어의 첫 걸음 단계

Pre-STARTER
초등 1,2학년
영어를 시작하는 단계

STARTER
초등 3,4학년
영어의 밑바탕을 다지는 단계

BASIC
초등 5,6학년
영어의 도약 단계

JUNIOR
중학생
영어의 실전 단계

HIGH JUNIOR
고등학생
영어의 고급화 단계

ADVANCED
대학생,직장인
영어의 완성 단계

TOSEL
교재 Series

TOSEL LEVEL	Age	Vocabulary Frequency	Readability Score	교과 과정 연계	Grammar	VOCA	Reading	Listening
Cocoon	K5-K7	500	0-1	Who is he? (국어 1단원 1-1)	There is · There are	150	Picking Pumpkins (Phonics Story)	Phonics
Pre-Starter	P1-P2	700	1-2	How old are you? (통합교과 1-1)	be + adjective	300	Me & My Family (Reading series Ch.1)	묘사하기
Starter	P3-P4	1000-2000	1-2	Spring, Summer, Fall, Winter (통합교과 3-1)	Simple Present	800	Ask More Questions (Reading Series Ch.1)	날씨/시간 표현
Basic	P5-P6	3000-4000	3-4	Show and Tell (사회 5-1)	Superlative	1700	Culture (Reading Series Ch.3)	상대방 의견 묻고 답하기
Junior	M1-M2	5000-6000	5-6	중 1, 2 과학, 기술가정	to-infinitive	4000	Humans and Animals (Reading Series Ch.1)	정보 묻고 답하기
High Junior	H1-H3	5000-6000	5-6	고등학교 - 체육	2nd Conditional	7000	Health (Reading Series Ch.1)	사건 묘사하기

- TOSEL의 세분화된 레벨은 각 연령에 맞는 어휘와 읽기 지능 및 교과 과정과의 연계가 가능하도록 설계된 교재들로 효과적인 학습 커리큘럼을 제공합니다.

- TOSEL의 커리큘럼에 따른 학습은 정확한 레벨링 → 레벨에 적합한 학습 → 영어 능력 인증 시험 TOSEL에서의 공신력 있는 평가를 통해 진단 → 학습 → 평가의 선순환 구조를 실현합니다.

About TOSEL®

TOSEL은 각급 학교 교과과정과 연령별 인지단계를 고려하여 단계별 난이도와 문항으로
영어 숙달 정도를 측정하는 영어 사용자 중심의 맞춤식 영어능력인증 시험제도입니다.
평가유형에 따른 개인별 장점과 단점을 파악하고, 개인별 영어학습 방향을 제시하는 성적분석자료를 제공하여
영어능력 종합검진 서비스를 제공함으로써 영어 사용자인 소비자와
영어능력 평가를 토대로 영어교육을 담당하는 교사 및 기관 인사관리자인 공급자를
모두 만족시키는 영어능력인증 평가입니다.

TOSEL은 인지적-학문적 언어 사용의 유창성 (Cognitive-Academic Language Proficiency, CALP)과
기본적-개인적 의사소통능력 (Basic Interpersonal Communication Skill, BICS)을
엄밀히 구분하여 수험자의 언어능력을 가장 친밀하게 평가하는 시험입니다.

대상	목적	용도
유아, 초, 중, 고등학생, 대학생 및 직장인 등 성인	한국인의 영어구사능력 증진과 비영어권 국가의 영어 사용자의 영어구사능력 증진	실질적인 영어구사능력 평가 + 입학전형 및 인재선발 등에 활용 및 직무역량별 인재 배치

연혁

2002.02	국제토셀위원회 창설 (수능출제위원역임 전국대학 영어전공교수진 중심)
2004.09	TOSEL 고려대학교 국제어학원 공동인증시험 실시
2006.04	EBS 한국교육방송공사 주관기관 참여
2006.05	민족사관고등학교 입학전형에 반영
2008.12	고려대학교 편입학시험 TOSEL 유형으로 대체
2009.01	서울시 공무원 근무평정에 TOSEL 점수 가산점 부여
2009.01	전국 대부분 외고, 자사고 입학전형에 TOSEL 반영 (한영외국어고등학교, 한일고등학교, 고양외국어고등학교, 과천외국어고등학교, 김포외국어고등학교, 명지외국어고등학교, 부산국제외국어고등학교, 부일외국어 고등학교, 성남외국어고등학교, 인천외국어고등학교, 전북외국어고등학교, 대전외국어고등학교, 청주외국어고등학교, 강원외국어고등학교, 전남외국어고등학교)
2009.12	청심국제중·고등학교 입학전형 TOSEL 반영
2009.12	한국외국어교육학회, 팬코리아영어교육학회, 한국음성학회, 한국응용언어학회 TOSEL 인증
2010.03	고려대학교, TOSEL 출제기관 및 공동 인증기관으로 참여
2010.07	경찰청 공무원 임용 TOSEL 성적 가산점 부여
2014.04	전국 200개 초등학교 단체 응시 실시
2017.03	중앙일보 주관기관 참여
2018.11	관공서, 대기업 등 100여 개 기관에서 TOSEL 반영
2019.06	미얀마 TOSEL 도입 발족식
	베트남 TOSEL 도입 협약식
2019.11	2020학년도 고려대학교 편입학전형 반영
2020.04	국토교통부 국가자격시험 TOSEL 반영
2021.07	소방청 간부후보생 선발시험 TOSEL 반영

What's TOSEL?

"Test of Skills in the English Language"

TOSEL은 비영어권 국가의 영어 사용자를 대상으로 영어구사능력을 측정하여
그 결과를 공식 인증하는 영어능력인증 시험제도입니다.

영어 사용자 중심의 맞춤식 영어능력 인증 시험제도

맞춤식 평가

획일적인 평가에서
세분화된 평가로의 전환

TOSEL은 응시자의 연령별
인지단계에 따라 별도의 문항과 난이도를
적용하여 평가함으로써 평가의
목적과 용도에 적합한 평가 시스템을
구축하였습니다.

공정성과 신뢰성 확보

국제토셀위원회의 역할

TOSEL은 고려대학교가 출제 및 인증기관
으로 참여하였고 대학입학수학능력시험
출제위원 교수들이 중심이 된
국제토셀위원회가 주관하여
사회적 공정성과 신뢰성을 확보한
평가 제도입니다.

수입대체 효과

외화유출 차단 및 국위선양

TOSEL은 해외시험응시로 인한 외화의
유출을 막는 수입대체의 효과를 기대할 수
있습니다. TOSEL의 문항과 시험제도는
비영어권 국가에 수출하여 국위선양에
기여하고 있습니다.

Why TOSEL® —— 왜 TOSEL인가

01 학교 시험 폐지

일선 학교에서 중간, 기말고사 폐지로 인해 객관적인 영어 평가 제도의 부재가 우려됩니다. 그러나 전국단위로 연간 4번 시행되는 TOSEL 평가시험을 통해 학생들은 정확한 역량과 체계적인 학습방향을 꾸준히 진단받을 수 있습니다.

02 연령별/단계별 대비로 영어학습 점검

TOSEL은 응시자의 연령별 인지단계 및 영어 학습 단계에 따라 총 7단계로 구성되었습니다. 각 단계에 알맞은 문항유형과 난이도를 적용해 모든 연령 및 학습 과정에 맞추어 가장 효율적으로 영어실력을 평가할 수 있도록 개발된 영어시험입니다.

03 학교내신성적 향상

TOSEL은 학년별 교과과정과 연계하여 학교에서 배우는 내용을 학습하고 평가할 수 있도록 문항 및 주제를 구성하여 내신영어 향상을 위한 최적의 솔루션을 제공합니다.

04 수능대비 직결

유아, 초, 중등시절 어렵지 않고 즐겁게 학습해 온 영어이지만, 수능시험준비를 위해 접하는 영어의 문항 및 유형 난이도에 주춤하게 됩니다. 이를 대비하기 위해 TOSEL은 유아부터 성인까지 점진적인 학습을 통해 수능대비를 자연적으로 해나갈 수 있습니다.

05 진학과 취업에 대비한 필수 스펙관리

개인별 '학업성취기록부' 발급을 통해 영어학업성취이력을 꾸준히 기록한 영어학습 포트폴리오를 제공하여 영어학습 이력을 관리할 수 있습니다.

06 자기소개서에 토셀 기재

개별적인 진로 적성 Report를 제공하여 진로를 파악하고 자기소개서 작성시 적극적으로 활용할 수 있는 객관적인 자료를 제공합니다.

07 영어학습 동기부여

시험실시 후 응시자 모두에게 수여되는 인증서는 영어학습에 대한 자신감과 성취감을 고취시키고 동기를 부여합니다.

08 AI 분석 영어학습 솔루션

국내외 15,000여 개 학교·학원 단체 응시인원 중 엄선한 100만 명 이상의 실제 TOSEL 성적 데이터를 기반으로 영어인증시험 제도 중 세계 최초로 인공지능이 분석한 개인별 AI 정밀 진단 성적표를 제공합니다. 최첨단 AI 정밀진단 성적표는 최적의 영어 학습 솔루션을 제시하여 영어 학습에 소요되는 시간과 노력을 획기적으로 절감해줍니다.

09 명예의 전당, 우수협력기관 지정

우수교육기관은 'TOSEL 우수 협력 기관'에 지정되고, 각 시/도별, 최고득점자를 명예의 전당에 등재합니다.

Evaluation ——————— 평가

평가의 기본원칙
TOSEL은 PBT(Paper Based Test)를 통하여 간접평가와 직접평가를 모두 시행합니다.

TOSEL은 언어의 네 가지 요소인 읽기, 듣기, 말하기, 쓰기 영역을 모두 평가합니다.

문자언어   음성언어

읽기능력 + 듣기능력
쓰기능력   말하기능력

대한민국 대표 영어능력 인증 시험제도

TOSEL®

Reading 읽기	모든 레벨의 읽기 영역은 직접 평가 방식으로 측정합니다.
Listening 듣기	모든 레벨의 듣기 영역은 직접 평가 방식으로 측정합니다.
Writing 쓰기	모든 레벨의 쓰기 영역은 간접 평가 방식으로 측정합니다.
Speaking 말하기	모든 레벨의 말하기 영역은 간접 평가 방식으로 측정합니다.

TOSEL은 연령별 인지단계를 고려하여 아래와 같이 7단계로 나누어 평가합니다.

1 단계	**TOSEL**® COCOON	5~7세의 미취학 아동
2 단계	**TOSEL**® Pre-STARTER	초등학교 1~2학년
3 단계	**TOSEL**® STARTER	초등학교 3~4학년
4 단계	**TOSEL**® BASIC	초등학교 5~6학년
5 단계	**TOSEL**® JUNIOR	중학생
6 단계	**TOSEL**® HIGH JUNIOR	고등학생
7 단계	**TOSEL**® ADVANCED	대학생 및 성인

Grade Report

성적표 및 인증서

개인 AI 정밀진단 성적표

십 수년간 전국단위 정기시험으로 축적된 빅데이터를 교육공학적으로 분석·활용하여 산출한 개인별 성적자료

정확한 영어능력진단 / 섹션별·파트별 영어능력 및 균형 진단 / 명예의 전당 등재 여부 / 온라인 최적화된 개인별 상세
성적자료를 위한 QR코드 / 응시지역, 동일학년, 전국에서의 학생의 위치

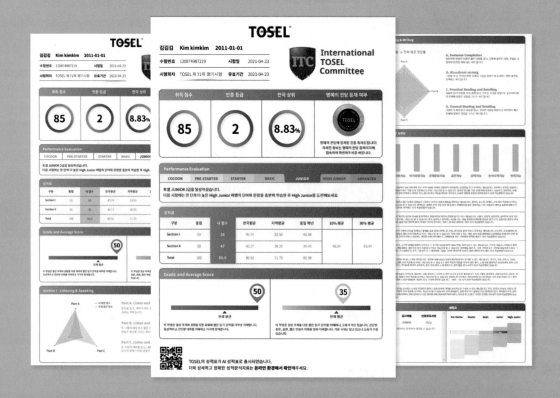

단체 및 기관 응시자 AI 통계 분석 자료

십 수년간 전국단위 정기시험으로 **축적된 빅데이터를**
교육공학적으로 분석·활용하여 산출한 응시자 통계 분석 자료

- 단체 내 레벨별 평균성적추이, LR평균 점수, 표준편차 파악
- 타 지역 내 다른 단체와의 점수 종합 비교 / 단체 내 레벨별
  학생분포 파악
- 동일 지역 내 다른 단체 레벨별 응시자의 평균 나이 비교
- 동일 지역 내 다른 단체 명예의 전당 등재 인원 수 비교
- 동일 지역 내 다른 단체 최고점자의 최고 점수 비교
- 동일 지역 내 다른 응시자들의 수 비교

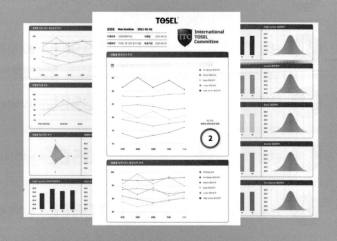

'토셀 명예의 전당' 등재

특별시, 광역시, 도 별 **1등** 선발
(7개시 9개도 **1등** 선발)

*홈페이지 로그인 - 시험결과 - 명예의 전당에서
해당자 등재 증명서 출력 가능

'학업성취기록부'에 토셀 인증등급 기재

개인별 **'학업성취기록부'** 평생 발급
진학과 취업을 대비한 **필수 스펙관리**

인증서

대한민국 초,중,고등학생의 영어숙달능력 평가 결과 공식인증

고려대학교 인증획득 (2010. 03)   팬코리아영어교육학회 인증획득 (2009. 10)   한국응용언어학회 인증획득 (2009. 11)

한국외국어교육학회 인증획득 (2009. 12)   한국음성학회 인증획득 (2009. 12)

TOSEL 시험을 기준으로 빈출 지표를 활용한 문법 선정 및 예문과 문제 구성

TOSEL 시험 활용

- 실제 TOSEL 시험에 출제된 빈출 문항을 기준으로 단계별 학습을 위한 문법 선정

- 실제 TOSEL 시험에 활용된 문장을 사용하여 예문과 문제를 구성

- 문법 학습 이외에 TOSEL 기출 문제 풀이를 통해서 TOSEL 및 실전 영어 시험 대비 학습

세분화된 레벨링

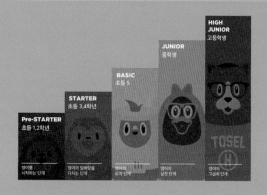

20년 간 대한민국 영어 평가 기관으로서

연간 4회 전국적으로 실시되는 정기시험에서

축적된 성적 데이터를 기반으로

정확하고 세분화된 레벨링을 통한

영어 학습 콘텐츠 개발

언어의 4대 영역 균형 학습 + 평가

1. TOSEL 평가: 학생의 영어 능력을 정확하게 평가

2. 결과 분석 및 진단: 시험 점수와 결과를 분석하여 학생의 강점, 취약점, 학습자 특성 등을 객관적으로 진단

3. 학습 방향 제시: 객관적 진단 데이터를 기반으로 학습자 특성에 맞는 학습 방향 제시 및 목표 설정

4. 학습: 제시된 방향과 목표에 따라 학생에게 적합한 문법 학습법 소개 및 영어의 체계와 구조 이해

5. 학습 목표 달성: 학습 후 다시 평가를 통해 목표 달성 여부 확인 및 성장을 위한 다음 학습 목표 설정

Grammar Series ——— Level

TOSEL의 Grammar Series는 레벨에 맞게 단계적으로
문법을 학습할 수 있도록 구성되어 있습니다.

Pre-Starter	Starter	Basic	Junior	High Junior

- 그림을 활용하여 문법에 대한 이해도 향상
- 다양한 활동을 통해 문법 반복 학습 유도
- TOSEL 기출 문제 연습을 통한 실전 대비

- TOSEL 기출의 빈도수를 활용한 문법 선정으로 효율적 학습
- 실제 TOSEL 지문의 예문을 활용한 실용적 학습 제공
- TOSEL 기출 문제 연습을 통한 실전 대비

최신 수능 출제
문법을 포함하여
수능 대비 가능

70분 학습 Guideline

01 Unit Intro

2분

■ 중등 교육과정에서 익혀야 하는 문법과 단어를 중심으로
단원의 문법에 대해 미리 생각해보기

02 개념

15분

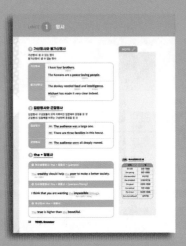

■ Unit Intro의 요약을 표로 구조화하여 세부적으로
학습하기 용이하게 구성

05 Sentence Completion

10분

■ Unit에서 배운 문법을 활용하여 문제 해결하기

■ 빈칸 채우기, 알맞은 표현 고르기 등 TOSEL 실전 문제 학습

■ 틀린 문제에 대해서는 해당 Unit에서 복습하도록 지도하기

06 Error Recognition

10분

■ 수능 유형의 실전 문제 학습을 통해 TOSEL 시험 뿐만 아니라
수능 영어 또한 대비 가능

■ 5개년 TOSEL 기출을 활용하여 더욱 생생한 문법

03
 Activity

3분

■ 배운 문법을 활용하여 문제 해결하기

■ Matching, O/X 활동을 하며
　문법의 기초 학습

04
Exercise

10분

■ 다양한 Exercise 활동을 하며 혼동하기 쉬운
　문법 학습

■ 문장 안에 문법적으로 알맞은 단어를 선택하거나
　쓰는 활동을 하며 혼동하기 쉬운 문법 학습

07
 Unit Review

10분

■ 빈칸을 채우는 형태로 구성하여 수업 시간 후
　복습에 용이하게 구성

■ 배운 문법을 활용하여 예시 문장을 직접 써보는 시간

08
TOSEL 실전문제

10분

■ 실제 TOSEL 기출 문제를 통한 실전 대비 학습

■ 실제 시험 시간과 유사하게 풀이할 수 있도록 지도하기

■ 틀린 문제에 대해서는 해당 단원에서 복습하도록 지도하기

PreStarter/Starter/Basic Syllabus

PreStarter		Basic		2015 개정 초등 영어 언어형식
Chapter	Unit	Chapter	Unit	
I. 명사: 명사는 이름이야	1 셀 수 있는 명사	I. 명사	1 셀 수 있는 명사 앞에 붙는 관사 the/a/an	**A** boy/The **boy**/The (two) boys ran in the park. **The** store is closed.
	2 셀 수 있는 명사 앞에 붙는 관사 a/an		2 셀 수 없는 명사를 측정하는 단위	**Water** is very important for life. **Kate** is from **London**.
	3 셀 수 없는 명사		3 규칙 복수명사	The **two boys** ran in the park.
	4 명사의 복수형		4 불규칙 복수명사	
II. 대명사: 명사를 대신하는 대명사	1 주격 대명사	II. 대명사	1 단수대명사의 격	**She** is a teacher, and **he**'s a scientist. I like **your** glasses. What about **mine**?
	2 소유격 대명사		2 복수대명사의 격	**They**'re really delicious. **We** are very glad to hear from him.
	3 목적격 대명사		3 1, 2인칭 대명사의 활용	**I** like math, but Susan doesn't like it. He will help **you**.
	4 지시대명사		4 3인칭 대명사의 활용	Which do you like better, **this** or **that**? **These** are apples, and **those** are tomatoes. **That** dog is smart. **These/Those** books are really large.
III. 형용사: 명사&대명사를 꾸미는 형용사	1 형용사의 명사수식	III. 동사	1 동사의 기본시제	He **walks** to school every day. We **played** soccer yesterday. She **is going to** visit her grandparents next week. He **is sleeping** now. I **will visit** America next year.
	2 형용사의 대명사수식		2 동사의 불규칙 과거형	
	3 숫자와 시간		3 헷갈리기 쉬운 동사	**It's half past four.** **What time** is it? I **don't** like snakes. We **didn't** enjoy the movie very much.
	4 지시형용사		4 조동사	She **can** play the violin. Tom **won't** be at the meeting tomorrow. I **will** visit America next year. You **may** leave now.

Junior **Syllabus**

High Junior **Syllabus**

High Junior		2015 개정 중등 영어 언어형식
Chapter	**Unit**	
I. 문장의 형성	1 8품사와 문장 성분	The audience is/are enjoying the show. I'd like to **write a diary**, but I'm too busy to do so. He**'s being** very rude. We **are hoping** you will be with us.
	2 문장의 형식	
	3 문장의 배열	I think **(that)** he is a good actor. **Although/Though** it was cold, I went swimming.
	4 문장의 강조	The weather was **so** nice **that** we went hiking. **It was Justin who/that** told me the truth.
II 부정사와 동명사	1 원형부정사	You shouldn't **let** him **go** there again. I **heard** the children **sing/singing**.
	2 to부정사	He seemed **to have been ill (for some time)**. Bill promised Jane **to work out with her**. I remembered **John/John's coming late for class**. It goes without **saying that time is money**. There is no use **crying over the spilt milk**.
	3 동명사	
	4 to부정사와 동명사구	
III. 분사	1 현재분사	At the station I met a lady **carrying a large umbrella**. **With the night coming**, stars began to shine in the sky.
	2 과거분사	Wallets **found on the street** must be reported to the police.
	3 분사구문	**Walking along the street**, I met an old friend. **Having seen that movie before**, I wanted to see it again.
	4 독립분사구문	**Joshua returning home**, the puppy ran toward him. **Frankly speaking**, I failed the test.
IV. 수동태	1 수동태의 형성	The building **was built** in 1880. I **was made** to clean the room. Nolan **was seen** to enter the building. The monkey **has been raised** by human parents for years. Cooper **will be invited** to today's meeting. The information superhighway **will have been introduced** to everyone by 2015.
	2 수동태와 능동태의 전환	
	3 수동태와 전치사의 사용	
	4 주의해야 할 수동태 용법	
V. 관계대명사와 관계부사	1 관계대명사의 사용	The girl **who is playing the piano** is called Ann. This is the book **(that) I bought yesterday**.
	2 관계대명사와 선행사	Please tell me **what happened**.
	3 관계대명사의 생략	This is **why** we have to study English grammar.
	4 관계부사	The town **in which I was born** is very small. That's just **how he talks**, always serious about his work.
VI. 가정법	1 가정법 현재와 과거	**If it were not for you, I would** be lonely.
	2 가정법 과거완료	**Had** I had enough money, I **would have bought** a cell phone. **Without/But for** your advice, I **would have** failed.
	3 혼합가정법	I **wish** I **had learned** swimming last summer. He acts **as if** he **had been** there.
	4 특수가정법	I'd **rather** we **had** dinner now. **Provided that/As long as** they had plenty to eat, the crew **seemed** to be happy.

CHAPTER 04

IV. 문장의 시제

UNIT 01

단순시제

생김새	**❶ 현재시제**: 동사원형 (주어가 3인칭 단수인 경우 '동사원형 + -(e)s') I **live** in Korea. **❷ 과거시제**: '동사원형 + -(e)d' I **lived** in Canada until last year. **❸ 미래시제**: 'will[shall] + 동사원형', 'be going to + 동사원형 등 I **will live** in the UK.
쓰임	**❶ 현재시제**: 현재의 상태, 습관적인 행위·동작, 불변의 진리·보편적 사실 등을 나타낼 때 불변의 진리: Water **freezes** at 0℃. **❷ 과거시제**: 과거의 동작·상태, 과거의 습관·반복적인 행위, 역사적 사실 등을 나타낼 때 과거의 습관: She usually **went** to bed late in those days. **❸ 미래시제**: 시간의 흐름에 따른 미래의 일(단순미래), 주어의 의지가 들어가는 미래의 일(의지미래)을 나타낼 때 단순미래: I **will be** fifteen next birthday.

1 현재시제

They **are** at home now. 현재의 상태

Here **com**es the bus! 말하는 순간과 동시 사건

She **run**s when she feels sad. 습관적인 행위 · 동작

The sun **ris**es in the east. 불변의 진리 · 보편적 사실

He **liv**es in Seoul. 무제한적 상태의 연속

It **say**s in the Bible, "love your neighbors." 역사적 현재 · 옛 서적에서의 인용

2 과거시제

I got up at six this morning. 과거 한 시점에서의 동작 · 상태

Last Tuesday, he **watch**ed TV all day long. 과거 특정 기간의 동작 · 상태

I usually went bed at twelve in those days. 과거의 습관 · 반복적인 행위

Columbus **reach**ed America in 1492. 역사적 사실

He said he would go there in a few days. 과거에서 본 미래

3 미래시제

단순미래	I will **be** twenty years old next year.
	He will **recover** soon.
의지미래	I will **give** you the money.
	Will you **do** me a favor?

✏️ Activity

각 단어를 알맞은 시제와 연결시키세요.

❶ are   •

❷ watched   •

❸ reached   •

❹ rise   •   •   (a) 현재시제

❺ will recover   •

                              •   (b) 과거시제

❻ reached   •

❼ is   •   •   (c) 미래시제

❽ will do   •

❾ loves   •

❿ lived   •

Exercise

Exercise 1

주어진 동사를 과거, 현재, 미래 중 가장 알맞은 것으로 바꿔 문장을 완성하세요.

❶ What _____ you _____ tomorrow? (do)

❷ I usually _____ dinner at 7 p.m. (have)

❸ The train _____ supposed to arrive here one hour ago. (be)

❹ The last bus _____ a minute ago. (leave)

❺ The amusement park _____ a festival to audience every night.

Exercise 2

둘 중 맞는 단어를 고르세요.

❶ Summer in Korea   was / is   very hot and   rains / rained   a lot.

❷ I wonder if Rachel   attends / will attend   the meeting tomorrow.

❸ We   spend / spent   an hour coming up with the solutions yesterday.

❹ The next train   arrive / will arrive   thirty minutes later.

❺ She currently   lived / lives   in Seoul.

 Exercise 3

보기에서 동사를 골라 가장 알맞은 시제로 바꿔 문장을 완성하세요.

| 보기 | ① play | ② clean | ③ sleep | ④ invent | ⑤ wear |

① Galileo는 2000년 전에 추를 발명하였다.

Galileo _____ the pendulum two thousand years ago.

② 프랑스 축구 팀은 크로아티아와 다음 달에 경기를 할 것이다.

The French soccer team _____ against Croatia next month.

③ 과거에, 여자아이들만 치마를 입었지만, 현재는 몇몇 남자아이들도 치마를 입는다.

In the past, only girls _____ skirts, but today, some boys do.

④ 오늘은 너무 바쁜 날이므로 내 방을 내일 청소할 것이다.

I _____ my room tomorrow since today is such a busy day.

⑤ 아기들은 첫번째 해에 하루의 대부분을 잠을 잔다.

Babies _____ for most of the day in the first year.

Sentence Completion

1 A : Where is Bob?

B : He _____ in the living room.

(A) be

(B) is

(C) was

(D) to be

2 A : Here _____ the queen! Hurry up!

B : Wait a minute. I am finishing this burger.

(A) come

(B) came

(C) comes

(D) coming

3 A : Did Emma _____ her present?

B : She loved it.

(A) enjoy

(B) enjoys

(C) enjoyed

(D) enjoying

4 A : What happened to your leg?

B : I _____ it when I fell off my bike.

(A) break

(B) broke

(C) breaks

(D) broken

5 A : _____ you do me a favor?

B : Sure. What is it?

(A) Are

(B) Did

(C) Will

(D) Does

6 My father _____ at a bank. My father is a banker.

(A) work

(B) works

(C) worked

(D) working

7 My hobby is reading books.

I _____ twelve books a month.

(A) read

(B) reads

(C) reading

(D) to read

8 My grandmother _____ in New York when she was 18.

(A) live

(B) lives

(C) lived

(D) living

9 The police _____ a serial killer yesterday.

(A) arrest

(B) arrested

(C) arresting

(D) to arrest

10 Jamie _____ take care of his dogs while he is gone.

(A) do

(B) will

(C) does

(D) going

Error Recognition

 틀린 문장 고르기

다음 중 문법적으로 틀린 것을 고르세요.

Sally **1** loves shopping. It's her favorite thing to do. She likes to shop with her friends at the mall. She can't go to the mall during the week because she's busy studying. Her mom only lets her shop on Saturdays. Last week, she **2** decide not to study on Friday. So, she went to the mall with her friends. Sally's mom saw her **3** at the mall and was very angry. Her mom told **4** her that she couldn't go shopping for one month! After this, Sally **5** learned to always listen to her mom.

 고쳐쓰기

틀린 문장을 쓰고 올바르게 고치세요.

→ _____

● TOSEL 기출문제 변형 수능/내신 출제유형

 틀린 문장 고르기

다음 중 문법적으로 틀린 것을 고르세요.

Last week, my class ① **went** on a field trip. We went to the town theater to watch a play written by William Shakespeare. When we got to the theater, we bought our tickets and found our seats. I had a really great seat in the front row. I loved ② **watching** the actors act. They were all so talented. And the make-up and costumes were ③ **amazingly** beautiful. Everyone in the audience stood up and clapped when the play ended. We clapped for two minutes! ④ **As** I walked home after school, I started to think about the play again. I was thinking how wonderful it was. So, I decided that I will ⑤ **tried** out for the school play. Auditions start next week!

 고쳐쓰기

틀린 문장을 쓰고 올바르게 고치세요.

 ➡ _____

Unit Review

✏️ 배운 내용 스스로 정리해보기

❶ 현재시제

현재시제는 ❶ [   ], ❷ 말하는 순간과 동시 사건, ❸ [   ],

❹ [   ], ❺ 무제한적 상태의 연속, ❻ 역사적 현재를 나타낼 때 쓴다.

예시문장 써보기

❶ [   ] → _____

❷ [   ] → _____

❸ [   ] → _____

❷ 과거시제

과거시제는 ❶ [   ], ❷ 과거 특정 기간에서의 동작·상태,

❸ 과거의 습관·반복적인 행위, ❹ [   ], ❺ [   ] 을(를) 나타낼 때 쓴다.

예시문장 써보기

❶ [   ] → _____

❷ [   ] → _____

❸ [   ] → _____

❸ 미래시제: 미래시제에는 ❶ [   ] 와 ❷ [   ] 가 있다.

예시문장 써보기

❶ [   ] → _____

❷ [   ] → _____

UNIT 02

진행시제

생김새	**①** **현재진행시제**: 'am[are, is] + -ing' Tom **is selling** goods. **②** **과거진행시제**: 'was[were] + -ing' He **was drawing** his portrait. **③** **미래진행시제**: 'will be + -ing' I **will be meeting** them at the office.
쓰임	**①** **현재진행시제**: 현재 진행 중인 동작, 반복적·일시적인 습관, 미래대용 등을 나타낼 때 We **are repairing** the cars. **②** **과거진행시제**: 과거 어느 시점의 진행 중인 동작, 과거의 미완료 동작, 과거 행위 중에 진행된 일, 과거에서 본 미래 등을 나타낼 때 They **were taking** pictures in the historic site. **③** **미래진행시제**: 미래 한 시점의 동작의 진행을 나타낼 때 The athlete **will be exercising** two hours later.

① 현재진행시제

He is reading a book now. 현재 진행 중인 동작

She is always finding fault with others. 반복적인 습관

I am getting up at six this month. 일시적인 습관

Their plane is departating at 10:00 tomorrow night. 미래대용

② 과거진행시제

What were you doing last night? 과거 어느 시점의 진행 중인 동작

He was making a boat several months ago. 과거의 미완료 동작

They were writing letters while I was cooking. 과거 행위 중에 진행된 일
= They wrote letters while I was cooking.
= They wrote letters while I cooked.

He was leaving for Paris the following day. 과거에서 본 미래

③ 미래진행시제

You will be studying here tomorrow. 미래 한 시점에서의 동작의 진행

✎ Activity

각 단어를 알맞은 시제와 연결시키세요.

1 is reading　•

2 were watching　•

3 was cooking　•

4 is finding　•　　　　　　•　(a) 현재진행시제

5 will be studying　•

　　　　　　　　　　　•　(b) 과거진행시제

6 am getting　•

7 was calling　•　　　　　•　(c) 미래진행시제

8 will be making　•

9 was leaving　•

10 are telling　•

Exercise

Exercise 1

괄호안에 알맞은 단어를 찾아 문장을 완성하세요.

❶ He **comes / is coming** from Seoul by bus now.

❷ Our teacher **gives / is giving** homework to us every day.

❸ She **is doing / does** her homework right now.

❹ He **is washing / washes** the dishes every day.

❺ She **listens / is listening** to music now.

Exercise 2

주어진 동사를 과거 혹은 과거진행으로 바꾸어 문장을 완성하세요.
(먼저 일어난 일은 과거진행, 나중에 일어난 일은 과거)

❶ She _____ science when I _____ her yesterday.
      (study)   (call)

❷ The new English teacher _____ me when I _____ to music.
               (call)   (listen)

❸ He _____ his homework when his mom _____ back home.
    (do)   (come)

❹ The couple first _____ each other when they _____ Barcelona.
        (meet)   (sightsee)

❺ They _____ with each other when she _____.
    (chat)   (cry)

✏ Exercise 3

주어진 동사를 미래진행으로 바꿔 문장을 완성하세요.

❶ I _____ alone when I arrive in London. (travel)

❷ She _____ the piano tomorrow afternoon. (play)

❸ While she will be watering the plants, I _____ my car. (wash)

❹ He _____ lunch at 2 p.m. since he has a lot of things to do. (have)

❺ I _____ in the cafe tomorrow. (study)

Sentence Completion

1 A : What are you doing right now?

B : I'm ⬚⬚⬚⬚⬚ pumpkin soup.

(A) cook

(B) cooks

(C) cooked

(D) cooking

4 A : What were you doing last night?

B : I was ⬚⬚⬚⬚⬚ my dog.

(A) walked

(B) walking

(C) to walking

(D) with walking

2 A : What's your plan after graduation?

B : I'm ⬚⬚⬚⬚⬚ to Chicago.

(A) move

(B) moving

(C) to moved

(D) to moving

5 A : What will you ⬚⬚⬚⬚⬚ at 8 p.m.?

B : I don't know. Maybe I will be taking a shower.

(A) doing

(B) can do

(C) be doing

(D) have done

3 A : I was ⬚⬚⬚⬚⬚ if you could help me with my homework.

B : I'd be happy to!

(A) wonder

(B) wonders

(C) wondered

(D) wondering

6 The audience are   for the pianist who played music wonderfully.

(A) claps

(B) clapped

(C) clapping

(D) have clapped

9 In the early 1800s, people were only   to research dinosaurs.

(A) starting

(B) to starting

(C) to be starting

(D) to be started

7 Modern artists are still   Persian miniatures today.

(A) paint

(B) painting

(C) to painting

(D) for painting

10 I will be   an Anti-Doping Awareness Workshop tomorrow at 6.

(A) give

(B) gave

(C) given

(D) giving

8 But the swimmers were   special swimsuits.

(A) wear

(B) wore

(C) worn

(D) wearing

Error Recognition

 틀린 문장 고르기

다음 중 문법적으로 틀린 것을 고르세요.

I had to go to the hospital today. I was at home in the backyard with my brother and we were ❶ **play** football. My brother threw me the ball and I caught it, ❷ **but** it hit my finger the wrong way. I dropped the ball and started yelling for my mother. She ran out of the house into the backyard. She took one look at my finger and said, "We're going to the hospital. Now!" I ❸ **was feeling** a little scared in the car on the way to the emergency room. I ❹ **thought** that maybe my finger, or even my hand, was broken. If that was true, then I ❺ **wouldn't** be able to play football for months.

 고쳐쓰기

틀린 문장을 쓰고 올바르게 고치세요.

 ➡ _____

● TOSEL 기출문제 변형 수능/내신 출제유형

 틀린 문장 고르기

다음 중 문법적으로 틀린 것을 고르세요.

> Skyscrapers are ❶ very tall buildings. They are so tall it looks like they ❷ touching the sky. One of the most famous skyscrapers in the world ❸ is the Empire State Building in New York City. The building has 102 ❹ floors and is 449 meters high. It is the tallest building in New York. There are only a few skyscrapers taller than Empire State Building. The tallest skyscraper in the world is ❺ in Taipei, Taiwan. It's called the Taipei 101 Building. It is 101 floors high and 509 meters tall.

 고쳐쓰기

틀린 문장을 쓰고 올바르게 고치세요.

_____

Unit Review

🖊 배운 내용 스스로 정리해보기

① <u>현재진행시제</u>

현재진행시제는 ❶ [＿＿＿＿＿＿＿＿＿], ❷ 반복적인 습관, ❸ 일시적인 습관,

❹ [＿＿＿＿] 을(를) 나타낼 때 쓴다.

예시문장 써보기

❶ [＿＿＿＿＿＿＿] → ＿＿＿＿＿＿＿＿＿＿＿＿＿＿

❷ [＿＿＿＿] → ＿＿＿＿＿＿＿＿＿＿＿＿＿＿＿

② <u>과거진행시제</u>

과거진행시제는 ❶ [＿＿＿＿＿＿＿＿＿＿], ❷ 과거의 미완료 동작,

❸ [＿＿＿＿＿＿＿＿], ❹ 과거에서 본 미래를 나타낼 때 쓴다.

예시문장 써보기

❶ [＿＿＿＿＿＿＿＿＿] → ＿＿＿＿＿＿＿＿＿＿＿

❷ [＿＿＿＿＿＿＿＿] → ＿＿＿＿＿＿＿＿＿＿＿＿

③ <u>미래진행시제</u>

미래진행시제는 [＿＿＿＿＿＿＿＿＿＿＿] 을(를) 나타낼 때 쓴다.

예시문장 써보기

[＿＿＿＿＿＿＿＿＿] → ＿＿＿＿＿＿＿＿＿＿＿＿

UNIT 03

완료시제

생김새	**현재완료시제: 'have[has] + p.p'** I **have** just **met** her.
용법	❶ **완료**: 과거에 시작한 일이 현재 완료되었음을 나타내며, 주로 already, yet, just, now 등과 함께 쓰임 I **have already finished** my work. ❷ **경험**: 과거부터 현재까지의 경험을 나타내며, 주로 ever, never, before 등과 함께 쓰임 I **have never been** there. ❸ **계속**: 과거의 동작·상태가 현재까지 계속됨을 나타내며, 주로 since, for 등과 함께 쓰임 I **have read** this book **since** last winter. ❹ **결과**: 과거의 동작·상태로 인한 결과가 현재에도 영향을 미침을 나타냄 He **has gone** to Korea.

UNIT 3 완료시제

1 현재완료의 일반용법

He has gone to America. 결과

I have been to the station. 완료

I have been to America. 경험

I have been in America. 계속

He has been in Seoul for three years. 계속

① 완료 (already, yet, just, now, lately, recently, today, etc.)

He has already finished his homework.

② 경험 (once, twice, often, ever, never, before, seldom, etc.)

I have watched a basketball game before.

③ 계속 (for, during, over, since, how long, etc.)

She has been in Seoul for 10 years.

④ 결과

My younger brother has lost his bicycle.

2 현재완료의 특별용법

since vs. for	We have lived here since 1992.
	We have lived here for two days.
ago vs. before	I met her two days ago. 명백한 과거이므로 과거시제와 결합
	I have met her before.
	I should have met her two days ago.

NOTE 🖊

TIP 현재완료의 특별용법

❶
since + 시점
for + 기간

❷
ago : 현재(기준점)로부터 ~전에
　　　지금으로부터 얼마 전에 일어난 일
　　　인지에 대해 말함
before : 과거, 미래(기준점)로부터 ~전에
　　　　정확히 시점은 모르고, 어느 때

✏️ Activity

각 문장의 현재 완료 용법을 파악해보세요.

| 보기 | ① 경험 | ② 결과 | ③ 완료 | ④ 계속 |

① He has been in London for two years. ( )

② I have been to Spain. ( )

③ My younger sister has lost her purse. ( )

④ They have already finished their team project. ( )

⑤ Carl has had the flu since last week. ( )

⑥ I have just arrived home. ( )

⑦ Have you ever built a house? ( )

⑧ He has just eaten breakfast. ( )

⑨ We have lived in Seoul since 2017. ( )

⑩ She has gone to Morocco. ( )

Exercise

 ## Exercise 1

주어진 동사를 현재완료로 바꿔 문장을 완성하세요.

❶ I _____ Chinese for ten years. (study)

❷ It is the first time I _____ him outside of the country. (ever, see)

❸ I _____ a lot of money to buy a new laptop. (already, save)

❹ She is a famous composer, and she _____ many songs so far. (write)

❺ He _____ a basketball game before. (watch)

 ## Exercise 2

둘 중 맞는 단어를 고르세요.

❶ He   had / has   already finished his assignment.

❷ I should have met her three days   ago / before   .

❸ My girlfriend   grew / has grown   flowers for five years.

❹ He has taken many photographs   so far / yesterday   .

❺ Have you seen a soccer match in the stadium   before / still   ?

 Exercise 3

밑줄 친 부분을 바르게 고쳐보세요.

❶ **Did you ever see** her before?

➡

❷ He **is studying** abroad for five years.

➡

❸ **How long are you waiting** for the train?

➡

❹ Today **I have read** the newspaper while eating breakfast.

➡

❺ I **am not seeing** the new film yet.

➡

Sentence Completion

1 A : Have you been to Ireland?

B : No, I've _____ been there before.

(A) no

(B) none

(C) never

(D) nowhere

2 A : I started doing my homework at 6:00 and it's already 9:00!

B : So you _____ done it for three hours?

(A) are

(B) been

(C) have

(D) were

3 A : Where do you want to go?

B : I have _____ been to Taiwan before. Let's go there.

(A) for

(B) yet

(C) ever

(D) never

4 A : Have you tried this food _____ ?

B : Yes. It was delicious and I loved it.

(A) ago

(B) after

(C) before

(D) across

5 A : How long have you two been married?

B : We have been married _____ 8 years.

(A) to

(B) for

(C) after

(D) since

6 People have _____ calling the years of 2008 and 2009 the "supersuit era."

(A) start

(B) starts

(C) started

(D) starting

9 Earth Day has become an international celebration _____ 1970.

(A) to

(B) for

(C) since

(D) across

7 Koreans have _____ mammals, birds, and reptiles as symbols in art.

(A) use

(B) used

(C) using

(D) are using

10 People with foreign accent syndrome can use an accent they have never heard _____ .

(A) ago

(B) for

(C) since

(D) before

8 The painting has _____ on the prince's boat.

(A) be

(B) was

(C) were

(D) been

Error Recognition

● TOSEL 기출문제 변형 수능/내신 출제유형

 틀린 문장 고르기

다음 중 문법적으로 틀린 것을 고르세요.

Lucas is an athlete. He loves to play all sports. His favorite sport is soccer, but he plays hockey the best. Lucas **①** **has play** on many teams, so he has made lots of good friends that like to play sports too. To stay healthy and in good shape, he likes to go for a run, **②** **with** friends every morning before school. After school, he goes to the gym and lifts weights. **③** **This** helps his muscles become stronger. Exercise is an important part of being healthy, but so is the diet. This is why Lucas **④** **makes** sure to eat lots of fruits and vegetables with breakfast, lunch, and dinner. Also, he **⑤** **makes sure** to drink at least eight glasses of water a day.

 고쳐쓰기

틀린 문장을 쓰고 올바르게 고치세요.

 _____

● TOSEL 기출문제 변형 수능/내신 출제유형

 틀린 문장 고르기

다음 중 문법적으로 틀린 것을 고르세요.

The Eiffel Tower is one of the most famous buildings in the world. It ❶ **was built** in Paris, France in 1887, but wasn't finished being built until 1889. Over the years, the tower ❷ **has have** many things happen to it. In 1902, the tower was hit by lightning and had to be fixed. In 1956, there was a fire in the tower ❸ **and** the tower had to be fixed again. Many people didn't want the tower to be built because they thought ❹ **that** it was ugly. Now, people from all over the world ❺ **visit** Paris to take in its beauty.

 고쳐쓰기

틀린 문장을 쓰고 올바르게 고치세요.

 ➡ _____

✏️ 배운 내용 스스로 정리해보기

① __현재완료의 일반용법__

현재완료의 용법에는 ❶ _____, ❷ _____, ❸ _____, ❹ _____ 이(가) 있다.

예시문장 써보기

❶ _____ ➜ _____

❷ _____ ➜ _____

❸ _____ ➜ _____

❹ _____ ➜ _____

② __현재완료의 특별용법__

❶ _____ 은(는) 특정 시점과 함께 쓰고,

❷ _____ 은(는) 특정 기간과 함께 쓴다.

❸ _____ 은(는) 명백한 과거이므로 과거시제와 결합하고,

❹ _____ 은(는) 현재완료 시제와 결합할 수 있다.

예시문장 써보기

❶ 현재완료시제와 _____ ➜ _____

❷ 현재완료시제와 _____ ➜ _____

❸ 과기시제와 _____ ➜ _____

❹ 현재완료시제와 _____ ➜ _____

UNIT 04

시간을 나타내는 접속사

❶ after: '~후에'의 의미로, 종속절에 완료시제가 쓰이지만

완료시제와 거의 함께 쓰지 않음

I set the table **after** he came home.

❷ before: '~전에'의 의미

Turn off the TV **before** you go out.

❸ when: '~할 때'의 의미로,

시간의 어느 한 지점을 말할 때 씀

Take off your cap **when** you enter the room.

❹ while: '~하는 동안'의 의미로,

시간의 지속(계속)을 말할 때 씀

I arrived at the train station **while** he was driving.

❺ as: '~할 때, ~하는 동안, ~함에 따라' 등의 의미

I like listening to music **as** I study math.

❻ till[until]: '~할 때까지'의 의미

The man waited for her **until** she came.

❼ once: '일단 ~하면'의 의미

Once you start, you have to finish it.

NOTE

after vs. **since**	I'll go <u>after</u> I **finish** [have **finish**ed] my work. <u>After</u> I came here, I <u>heard</u> nothing. = <u>Since</u> I came here, I <u>have heard</u> nothing. Since는 계속의 뜻을 포함하므로 완료형과 쓰임
Before vs. **rather** **than**	It will be long <u>before</u> he notices it. It will **not** be long <u>before</u> spring comes. I will die <u>before</u> I surrender. = I will <u>rather</u> die <u>than</u> surrender.
when vs. **while**	Take off your shoes <u>when</u> you enter the room. He came <u>while</u> we <u>were **hav**ing</u> lunch. ≠ He came <u>while</u> we <u>had</u> lunch. (X) 계속적 의미가 없으므로 틀린 표현임 ≠ He came <u>while</u> we <u>were **hav**ing</u> lunch <u>for an hour.</u> (X) while이하의 절에서 계속을 나타내는 부사(구)는 쓸 수 없음
as	She sang <u>as</u> she cleaned her desk.
since	I <u>have seen</u> him twice <u>since</u> I <u>came</u> to Korea. = I <u>have seen</u> him twice <u>since</u> I <u>have come</u> to Korea. 현재까지의 계속을 명시하는 경우
till **[until]**	I'll wait here <u>until</u> you come back. We do not know the value of health <u>until</u> we lose it. = <u>Not until</u> we lose health <u>do we know</u> its value. = <u>It's</u> <u>not until</u> we lose health <u>that</u> we know its value.
once	<u>Once</u> you come, the rest is not a problem.
as **soon** **as**	He went home <u>as soon as</u> he got the phone call.

Activity

각 접속사를 알맞은 뜻과 연결시키세요.

❶ since

❷ when

❸ while

❹ before

❺ as soon as

❻ till

❼ as

(a) ...하자마자

(b) ... 하는 동안

(c) ...하면서

(d) ...한 이후로

(e) ...까지

(f) ...하기 전에

(g) ...하는 때

Exercise

Exercise 1

둘 중 맞는 단어를 고르세요.

① Call me **till / as soon as** you arrive in Paris.

② Make sure the lights are off **before / after** you go to bed.

③ Please do the laundry **as soon as / while** I am washing the dishes.

④ She kept talking **before / until** she ran out of breath.

⑤ I will die **after / before** I surrender.

Exercise 2

보기에서 알맞은 접속사를 골라 문장을 완성하세요.

| 보기 | ① while | ② when | ③ until | ④ once | ⑤ as |

① _____ I exercise, I usually run along the river.

② I will stay at home _____ the rain stops.

③ She was sleeping _____ I was doing my homework.

④ She studied math _____ she listened to music.

⑤ _____ you submit the assignment, you can't revise it anymore.

Exercise 3

빈칸에 알맞은 접속사를 써 넣으세요.

① Jacob은 소년일 때 부터 식물들에 대해 공부했다.

Jacob has studied plants _____ he was a boy.

② 빌딩에 들어가기 전에 나에게 전화하는 것을 잊지 마라.

Don't forget to call me _____ you enter the building.

③ 그녀가 돌아오면 우리는 영화를 보러 갈 것이다.

We will go to the movies _____ she gets back.

④ 그 소녀는 어두워질 때까지 공원에서 춤을 췄다.

The girl danced in the park _____ it got dark.

⑤ 수업이 시작하자마자, 그가 교실에 들어왔다.

_____ the class started, he entered the classroom.

Sentence Completion

1 A : Come back home _____ your father arrives.

B : Okay, mom.

(A) since

(B) when

(C) while

(D) before

2 A : _____ you open the lid, you have to eat the jam in two weeks.

B : Okay, I'll try.

(A) As

(B) Until

(C) Once

(D) Since

3 A : Where is Jane? I need to see her.

B : She left _____ the class finished.

(A) as

(B) once

(C) when

(D) as soon as

4 A : My brother is so annoying. He always sings _____ he is taking a shower.

B : You should talk to him.

(A) until

(B) when

(C) while

(D) as soon as

5 A : Seoul changed so much _____ I started to live in Korea.

B : Yeah, I agree.

(A) as

(B) since

(C) rather than

(D) as soon as

6 _____ Italian audience first heard this piece in 1725, it was completely new.

(A) When
(B) While
(C) Since
(D) Before

7 _____ music words end with '-issimo,' it means 'very.'

(A) While
(B) When
(C) Since
(D) Before

8 He worked as a clerk _____ he wrote to Professor Hardy.

(A) as
(B) until
(C) since
(D) while

9 Classical music was then used to relax the cows _____ they were being milked.

(A) as
(B) till
(C) once
(D) while

10 _____ Mau grew older, the lifestyle of his people on Satawal began to change.

(A) As
(B) Until
(C) While
(D) Since

Error Recognition

 틀린 문장 고르기

다음 중 문법적으로 틀린 것을 고르세요.

---

❶ **When** I was younger, my favorite time of the week was Saturday mornings. I really enjoyed waking up ❷ **early** on Saturdays. I would go down stairs and make a big bowl of cereal to eat for breakfast. Then, I would go and sit in front of the TV in the living room and watch cartoons ❸ **when** I was eating breakfast. I'm older now, so I'm busier on the weekends. I don't have the time to stay in my pajamas and watch cartoons. Now, I wake up and go to work. I have to work on Saturdays at my part-time job. ❹ **On** Sundays, I have to study and do my homework. I ❺ **like** my life now, but sometimes I wish I was young again.

 고쳐쓰기

틀린 문장을 쓰고 올바르게 고치세요.

● TOSEL 기출문제 변형 수능/내신 출제유형

 틀린 문장 고르기

다음 중 문법적으로 틀린 것을 고르세요.

> I have a pet bird named Willy. I've had him **①** **after** I was 4 years old. I taught eating from my hand **②** **to him** and saying "Pretty Bird". It's my job to clean his cage and to make sure he always has clean water. My little sister likes to play with my bird. I only let her play with him **③** **while** I am watching. She is too young to play with him alone. I'm afraid that she'll **④** **leave** his cage door open and he'll fly away. Willy is **⑤** **my** only pet and I love him. I will always do my best to make sure he is happy and healthy!

 고쳐쓰기

 틀린 문장을 쓰고 올바르게 고치세요.

➡ _____

Unit Review

✎ 배운 내용 스스로 정리해보기

시간을 나타내는 접속사

시간을 나타내는 접속사의 종류에는

❶ after, ❷   , ❸ before, ❹ rather than, ❺ when, ❻   ,

❼   , ❽   , ❾   , ❿   등이 있다.

예시문장 써보기

❶   → _____

❷   → _____

❸   → _____

❹   → _____

❺   → _____

❻   → _____

연습하기

괄호 안에서 빈칸에 알맞은 단어를 골라 써넣으세요.

❶ My father always calls me   his team wins the game. (when / while)

❷   Peter has a job, he can afford to buy a car. (Since / Before)

❸ You're not going out   you've finished this. (as / until)

❹ You can go swimming   I'm having lunch. (after / while)

❺   the show gains popularity, more tickets are sold daily. (As / Till)

❻ Don't forget to close the window   you go out. (ago / before)

TOSEL 실전문제 ④

PART 6. Sentence Completion

DIRECTIONS: In this portion of the test, you will be given 10 incomplete sentences. From the choices provided, choose the word or words that correctly complete the sentence. Then, fill in the corresponding space on your answer sheet.

1. A: I want to run around the track.
    B: Let's do it together! I usually _____ in my free time.

    (A) run
    (B) runs
    (C) is running
    (D) have been running

2. A: What will you do tomorrow?
    B: I _____ swimming with my cousin sister.

    (A) go
    (B) went
    (C) goes
    (D) will go

3. A: Where is Susan? I need to talk to her.
    B: She _____ her client now, so she's not available.

    (A) met
    (B) will meet
    (C) is meeting
    (D) has been meeting

4. A: _____ you ever been to Paris? It's amazing.
    B: Sadly, no. I really want to go there someday.

    (A) Are
    (B) Have
    (C) Were
    (D) Having never

5. A: I think she is a really cheerful person.
    B: I agree. She always sings _____ she walks.

    (A) as
    (B) till
    (C) after
    (D) as soon as

6. King Sejong _____ the language of Joseon dynasty in 1443.

   (A) invents
   (B) invented
   (C) will invent
   (D) is inventing

9. I will watch a movie and relax today. I have _____ finished all the work.

   (A) for
   (B) since
   (C) before
   (D) already

7. Joseph _____ in a hockey tournament three days later.

   (A) participate
   (B) participated
   (C) have participated
   (D) will be participating

10. The dog will wait here standing still _____ the dog owner comes back.

   (A) until
   (B) since
   (C) before
   (D) as soon as

8. Yesterday, my husband was cooking dinner while I _____ the floor.

   (A) will mop
   (B) is mopped
   (C) was mopping
   (D) have been mopped

Error Recognition

 1. 다음 중 문법적으로 틀린 것을 골라 고치세요.

● TOSEL 기출문제 변형 수능/내신 출제유형

1

> As humans ❶ **will get** older, they tend to slow down and age, until eventually they just stop. Most animals ❷ **do** the same thing, but some animals don't seem to get older at all. Lobsters, turtles and clams are among the animals that don't die from old age. These animals only ❸ **die** from disease or accidents.

 _____

2. 다음 밑줄 친 부분을 바르게 고치세요.

● TOSEL 기출문제 변형 수능/내신 출제유형

2

For almost five thousand years, the Great Pyramid of Giza **was** one of the most amazing buildings the world. There were three smaller pyramids nearby for his wives. Two rooms inside the pyramid were once filled with treasure, but thieves stole all of it long ago. It was originally 150 meters tall and took twenty years to build. Today, there are much taller buildings in the world, but the Pyramid of Giza is still amazing to look at.

 _____

CHAPTER 05

UNIT 01

to부정사

생김새	**'to+동사원형'** I studied hard <u>to **pass**</u> the exam.
쓰임	❶ **명사**: to부정사는 명사처럼 문장에서 주어·보어·목적어로 쓰일 수 있음 　주어: <u>To **eat**</u> fast is bad for your health. 　보어: My dream is <u>to **be**</u> a singer. 　목적어: She decided <u>to **go**</u> outside. ❷ **형용사**: to부정사는 형용사처럼 명사 · 대명사를 수식하거나 보어 자리에 놓여 서술어 역할을 함 　명사수식: I know the way <u>to **make**</u> lasagna. 　서술어 역할: She is <u>to **publish**</u> her new book. ❸ **부사**: to부정사는 부사처럼 형용사, 부사, 동사를 수식함 　형용사 수식: This question is hard <u>to **answer**</u>. 　동사 수식: We booked the restaurant <u>to **have**</u> her birthday party.

1 to부정사의 생김새

'to + 동사원형' 형태로 쓴다.

> I like <u>to **draw**</u> portraits of my friends.
>
> Kevin required me <u>to **do**</u> the dishes.
>
> <u>To **escape**</u> from here means we cooperate.

2 to부정사의 쓰임

명사	<u>To **have**</u> your dream is a wonderful thing. 주어 Her only fault is <u>to **talk**</u> too much. 주격 보어 Practice enabled him <u>to **win**</u> the race. 목적격 보어 I agreed <u>to **try**</u> a coconut ice cream. 목적어
형용사	I have no <u>friends</u> <u>to **eat**</u> dinner with. 명사 수식 The rumor <u>proved</u> <u>to **be**</u> false. 서술어 역할
부사	We were <u>frustrated</u> <u>to **hear**</u> the news. 형용사 수식 They planned a project <u>only</u> <u>to **fail**</u>. 부사 수식 Susan <u>went</u> home <u>to **get**</u> her coat. 동사 수식

Activity

각 문장에서 to부정사의 쓰임을 찾아보세요.

1 To have your dream is a wonderful thing. ( )

2 I don't have any paper to use. ( )

3 We were happy to hear the news. ( )

4 I agreed to try a chocolate ice cream. ( )

5 She went home to get his bag. ( )

6 I want to buy a laptop. ( )

7 It is easy to solve that problem. ( )

8 He needs a pen to write with. ( )

9 I should bring something to wear since it's cold. ( )

10 I waited all day long to buy the concert ticket. ( )

Exercise

 ## Exercise 1

괄호 안에서 알맞은 것을 찾아보세요.

❶ My father required me **to do / to doing** the dishes.

❷ They seem **to be enjoying / to enjoying** the music class.

❸ **To escape / Escape** from here means we cooperate.

❹ I like **to draw / drew** portraits of my parents.

❺ It's difficult **to find / find** rare diamonds.

 ## Exercise 2

괄호에서 알맞은 것을 고르고, to부정사가 답이라면 그 쓰임을 말해보세요.

❶ The students need a new gym **to play in / play** .

❷ I was foolish **to go out / go out** in this heavy rain.

❸ His goal is **to get / get** the top score in the quiz.

❹ She was determined **not to make / do not make** the same mistake again.

❺ I have no friends **to eat / eat** lunch with.

Exercise 3

보기에서 알맞은 동사를 골라 to부정사로 바꾸어 문장을 완성하세요.

보기 ① ask ② donate ③ become ④ write ⑤ fire ⑥ be

① 그의 꿈은 의사가 되는 것이다.
His dream is _____ a doctor.

② 형편이 어려운 사람들에게 기부를 하다니 너는 정말 너그러운 사람이구나.
It was very generous of you _____ money for the underprivileged.

③ 교수님께 추천서를 써달라고 부탁드리는 일은 어려운 일이다.
It is difficult _____ a professor _____ a recommendation letter.

④ Jacob은 자라서 간부가 되었다.
Jacob grew up _____ an executive.

⑤ 그 사장님은 이번 해에 그의 직원들을 해고하지 않기로 결정했다.
The boss chose _____ his employees this year.

Sentence Completion

❶ A : Why did my brother call?

   B : He called   tell you that he will visit.

(A) to

(B) for

(C) that

(D) while

❷ A : What do you usually like to do on weekends?

   B : I like   stay at home on weekends.

(A) so

(B) do

(C) be

(D) to

❸ A : I'm starving.

   B : What do you want   for dinner?

(A) eat

(B) ate

(C) to eat

(D) eating

❹ A : Is Laura coming today?

   B : No, she couldn't find someone   her daughter tonight.

(A) babysit

(B) to babysit

(C) babysitting

(D) was babysitting

❺ A : Wow, why did you buy all these onions?

   B : I bought these   onion rings for the party.

(A) make

(B) making

(C) to make

(D) be making

6 After All Ball died, Koko used sign language ⬚⬚⬚⬚⬚ get other pets and to talk to humans.

(A) by
(B) to
(C) so
(D) for

7 Scientists want ⬚⬚⬚⬚⬚ learn how this animal behavior is connected to earthquakes.

(A) to
(B) for
(C) with
(D) from

8 ⬚⬚⬚⬚⬚ your cat or dog, you can prepare an emergency box of supplies.

(A) Protect
(B) Protecting
(C) Protected
(D) To protect

9 Long before we had the Internet, we used messenger pigeons ⬚⬚⬚⬚⬚ notes.

(A) deliver
(B) delivering
(C) to deliver
(D) have deliver

10 Using this proper form ⬚⬚⬚⬚⬚ sit-ups can strengthen your stomach muscles.

(A) do
(B) did
(C) done
(D) to do

Error Recognition

● TOSEL 기출문제 변형 수능/내신 출제유형

 틀린 문장 고르기

다음 중 문법적으로 틀린 것을 고르세요.

Yesterday I went **①** **to** school by bus. It was a very long bus ride. I was on the bus for more than 30 minutes! By the time I got to school my teacher had already started **②** **teaching** . She was a little bit angry at me **③** **because** I was late. She said, "Tommy, next time you should leave earlier." I knew she was right so I said, "You're right, Mrs. Henderson. Next time, I promise **④** **to leave** earlier. I'll try not **⑤** **be** late again."

 고쳐쓰기

틀린 문장을 쓰고 올바르게 고치세요.

  _____

 ## 틀린 문장 고르기

다음 중 문법적으로 틀린 것을 고르세요.

My mom loves her garden. It is very big and beautiful. She has many **❶ different** kinds of plants and flowers growing in her garden. The sunflowers are the tallest flowers in the garden. They are much taller than the tulips. Maybe the tulips are shorter, **❷ but** I think they are prettier than the sunflowers. My favorite thing **❸ to done** in my mom's garden is **❹ to talk** to the flowers. I think it helps them **❺ to grow** big and strong!

 ## 고쳐쓰기

틀린 문장을 쓰고 올바르게 고치세요.

 ➡ _____

Unit Review

✏️ **배운 내용 스스로 정리해보기**

① to부정사의 생김새

to부정사는 ❶ [   ] 형태로 쓴다.

to부정사 형태로 바꾸어 영작하기

❶ meet ➜ _____

❷ teach ➜ _____

② to부정사의 쓰임

to부정사는 ❶ [   ], ❷ [   ], ❸ [   ] 처럼 쓰일 수 있다.

예시문장 써보기

❶ [   ] 적 용법 ➜ _____

❷ [   ] 적 용법 ➜ _____

❸ [   ] 적 용법 ➜ _____

UNIT 02

동명사

생김새	**'동사원형 + -ing'** I enjoy **spend**ing time with my friends.
쓰임	**동사의 성질을 가지고 명사의 역할을 함** ❶ **주어:** ~하는 것은 **Eat**ing slowly is good for your health. ❷ **목적어:** ~하는 것을 I finished **wrapp**ing her present. ❸ **보어:** ~하는 것이다 Her habit is **read**ing a lot of books.

① 동명사의 생김새

'동사원형 + -ing' 형태로 쓴다.

> I like **draw**ing portraits of my friends.
>
> **Escap**ing from here means we cooperate.

NOTE ✐

② 동명사의 쓰임

주어	**Hav**ing your dream is a wonderful thing. 주어
목적어	She finally quit **work**ing at the age of 76. 목적어 I have no friends who **enjoy eat**ing dinner with me. 타동사의 목적어
보어	Her only fault is **talk**ing too much. 주격 보어

✏ Activity

각 문장에서 동명사의 쓰임을 찾아보세요.

❶ Having your dream is a wonderful thing. (   )

❷ Her only fault is talking too much. (   )

❸ The police arrested him for speeding. (   )

❹ You should give up playing games for a good grade. (   )

❺ Wearing perfume makes her feel fresh. (   )

❻ I enjoy teaching grammar. (   )

❼ She is addicted to losing her weight. (   )

❽ Being a lawyer is a difficult process. (   )

❾ What I like the most is traveling around the world. (   )

❿ He should be ashamed of being bad-mannered. (   )

Exercise

 Exercise 1

둘 중 맞는 단어를 고르세요.

❶ My family postponed   **departing / departed**   for France.

❷   **Travel / Traveling**   by bicycle is very fun.

❸ Her hobby is   **bake / baking**   a bread.

❹ He is proud of his daughter   **is / being**   smart.

❺ My grandmother enjoys   **knitting / knitted**   a hat in her free time.

 Exercise 2

보기에서 알맞은 동사를 골라 동명사로 바꿔 문장을 완성하세요.

보기   **❶** build   **❷** finish   **❸** become   **❹** answer   **❺** see

❶ 그녀의 꿈은 잘 알려진 시인이 되는 것이다.
Her dream is _____ a well-known poet.

❷ 새로운 집을 짓는 것은 많은 노력을 요구한다.
_____ a new house requires a lot of effort.

❸ 그는 그 콘서트를 그녀와 보게 되는 것에 신이 났다.
He is excited about _____ the concert with her.

❹ 그녀가 그 프로젝트를 끝내는 것에 책임이 있다.
She is in charge of _____ the project.

❺ 사장님께서는 나에게 재정 사항에 대해 대답하는 것을 피하라고 지시하셨다.
The boss ordered me to avoid _____ about financial issues.

 Exercise 3

밑줄 친 부분이 틀리면 바르게 고치세요.

---

① **Play** basketball makes me feel happy.

➡

② Her hobby is **writing** poems.

➡

③ He enjoys **drinks** coffee every morning.

➡

④ I suggested **opened** a new banking account to him.

➡

⑤ Grace looks forward **to see** her cousin.

➡

Sentence Completion

❶ A : What do you do for fun?

B : I like _____ and playing the guitar.

(A) swim

(B) swam

(C) swimming

(D) is swimming

❷ A : Did you enjoy _____ a horse?

B : Yeah, it was fun.

(A) ride

(B) riding

(C) to ride

(D) to be riding

❸ A : _____ on the railing is dangerous! Come down here!

B : Sorry, I didn't know.

(A) Lean

(B) Leaned

(C) Leaning

(D) To leaning

❹ A : Robin, what is your dream?

B : My dream is _____ a dancer.

(A) becoming

(B) to becoming

(C) have become

(D) have becoming

❺ A : I think I should give up _____ cigarettes.

B : That's a good idea. Smoking is bad for your health.

(A) smoke

(B) smoking

(C) to smoke

(D) to be smoking

6 Whatever the reason, any athlete considering _____ should know that it is cheating.

(A) dope
(B) doping
(C) to dope
(D) to doping

9 In 1981, she heard that her 99-year-old grandfather was sick. She began _____ a letter to him.

(A) wrote
(B) written
(C) writing
(D) to written

7 _____ them required careful hands and a fine paint brush.

(A) Make
(B) Made
(C) Making
(D) To making

10 _____ future weather is one way we use statistics daily.

(A) Predict
(B) Predicted
(C) Predicting
(D) To Predicting

8 Music lovers enjoyed _____ a barking dog, chirping birds, and crackling fire in the form of a song.

(A) hearing
(B) to hear
(C) to hearing
(D) be hearing

UNIT 2 동명사

Error Recognition

 틀린 문장 고르기

다음 중 문법적으로 틀린 것을 고르세요.

I study hard in school because I want **①** **to be** a teacher. My favorite subjects are science, English, **②** **and** history. My friends get angry with me because sometimes I don't want to go outside and play. I like **③** **to stay** inside and do my homework. When I finish my homework, my mom lets me use the computer. I can play fun games that teach **④** **me** new things about my favorite subjects. I love **⑤** **learn** new things!

 고쳐쓰기

틀린 문장을 쓰고 올바르게 고치세요.

⬛⬛⬛⬛⬛⬛⬛   _____

틀린 문장 고르기

다음 중 문법적으로 틀린 것을 고르세요.

There are many different ways ❶ to communicate with people. My favorite is email. I check my email twice a day. It's easy ❷ to talk to friends and family that live far away by email. It's much quicker than writing a letter and ❸ take it to the post office. My grandmother is the only person in the family who doesn't use email. She doesn't own a computer. I think she'd like an email ❹ if she tried it. She says she prefers to write letters on pretty paper. She told ❺ me she thinks her letters are worth the wait. I agree!

 고쳐쓰기

틀린 문장을 쓰고 올바르게 고치세요.

➡

✎ 배운 내용 스스로 정리해보기

❶ 동명사의 생김새

동명사는 ❶ [   ] 형태로 쓴다.

동명사 형태로 바꾸어 영작하기

❶ drink → _____

❷ travel → _____

❷ 동명사의 쓰임

동명사는 동사의 성질을 가지고 명사의 역할을 하므로 ❶ [   ], ❷ [   ],

❸ [   ] (으)로 쓰일 수 있다.

예시문장 써보기

❶ [   ] → _____

❷ [   ] → _____

❸ [   ] → _____

UNIT 03

---

to부정사와 동명사의 비교

생김새	**❶ to부정사:** 'to + 동사원형' We have practiced hard to win the game. **❷ 동명사:** '동사원형 + -ing' I enjoy cooking.
의미	**❶ to부정사:** 앞으로의 일 Don't forget to close the door. **❷ 동명사:** 지난 일 I forgot closing the door.
쓰임	**❶ to부정사만을 취하는 동사:** ask, decide, want, expect 등 He asked me to borrow my book. **❷ 동명사만을 취하는 동사:** enjoy, finish, mind, avoid 등 Do you mind opening the window?

1 **의미와 관련한 차이**

❶ 부정사 (구체적: particular) vs. 동명사 (일반적: general)

I like <u>to</u> **swim** now. 구체적, 일시적 진술

I like **swimm**ing. 일반적, 습관적 진술
= I enjoy **swimm**ing.

❷ 부정사 (앞으로의 일: future) vs. 동명사 (지난 일: past)

I remember <u>to</u> **see** you tomorrow. 앞으로 해야 할 일을 기억

I remember **see**ing you yesterday. 지난 일을 기억

❸ 부정사 (가정적: hypothetical) vs. 동명사 (사실적: factual)

<u>To</u> **pass** the test can make her happy. 실제 합격한 것은 아님

Passing the test made her happy. 실제 합격한 사실

2 **to부정사 · 동명사만을 취하는 동사**

to부정사	I **asked** him <u>to</u> **bring** my wallet. 소망 · 기대
	Vanessa **decided** <u>to</u> **buy** the ticket. 약속 · 결심
	We **prepared** <u>to</u> **move** to another city. 노력 · 준비
	He **hesitates** <u>to</u> **learn** a new language. 기타
동명사	I **understand** her **forgett**ing it. 회상 · 후회 · 숙고 · 용서
	Mr. Pepper **admitted** his **be**ing careless. 인정 · 부인 · 변명
	They **allowed** my **leav**ing earlier. 기정 사실

Activity

각 동사가 목적어로 취하는 것과 연결시켜보세요.

① **ask** ·

② **understand** ·

③ **allow** ·

④ **admit** ·

⑤ **decide** · · **(a) to 부정사**

⑥ **prepare** ·

· **(b) 동명사**

⑦ **remember** ·

⑧ **hesitate** ·

⑨ **avoid** ·

⑩ **expect** ·

Exercise

 ## Exercise 1

괄호에서 알맞은 것을 모두 고르세요.

❶ He kept **to talk / talking** about what he bought yesterday.

❷ She wants **to make / making** a lunch reservation for her parents.

❸ Doctors should continue **to study / studying** about the latest treatments.

❹ Your kids should avoid **to eat / eating** junk food!

❺ I decided **to buy / buying** a new coat.

 ## Exercise 2

보기에서 알맞은 동사를 골라 to부정사 또는 동명사로 바꿔 문장을 완성하세요.

보기　　❶ correct　　❷ exercise　　❸ persuade　　❹ learn　　❺ leave

❶ 그들은 내가 더 일찍 떠나는 것을 허락했다.
They allowed my _____ earlier.

❷ 그녀는 새로운 언어를 배우는 것을 망설이지 않는다.
She does not hesitate _____ a new language.

❸ 나는 내 과제에서의 잘못된 부분을 바로잡으라고 지시받았다.
I was ordered _____ my mistakes in my assignment.

❹ 나는 그가 그 시험에 대한 공부를 하도록 설득하는 것을 포기했다.
I gave up _____ him to study for the exam.

❺ 그 의사는 내게 규칙적으로 운동할 것을 조언했다.
The doctor advised me _____ regularly.

 Exercise 3

주어진 동사를 to부정사 또는 동명사로 바꿔 문장을 완성하세요.

❶ I agreed _____ some money to the poor. (donate)

❷ The thief denied _____ taken the bag from her. (have)

❸ She truly enjoys _____ shopping every weekend. (go)

❹ He tried to persuade me _____ in French class. (enroll)

❺ He considers _____ seriously because of his health problem. (resign)

Sentence Completion

① A : Don't forget _____ the window before leaving the car.

B : Okay, mom.

(A) close
(B) closing
(C) to close
(D) to closing

② A : Remember _____ an umbrella on Thursday.

B : Why? Is it going to rain that day?

(A) bring
(B) brining
(C) brought
(D) to bring

③ A : Do you play the violin?

B : I used to, but not anymore. I stopped _____ it.

(A) play
(B) played
(C) to play
(D) playing

④ A : What kind of computer games do you play?

B : I enjoy _____ role-playing games.

(A) play
(B) plays
(C) to play
(D) playing

⑤ A : What did the manager say?

B : She decided _____ go of more people this year.

(A) let
(B) to let
(C) letting
(D) have let

6 _____ sick with the flu or other illnesses can be risky when it comes to superbug infections.

(A) Be
(B) Was
(C) Being
(D) To be

9 Avoid _____ towels with other people when you have an athlete's foot.

(A) share
(B) sharing
(C) to share
(D) was sharing

7 I remember _____ you for the first time. You were wearing a white dress.

(A) met
(B) meet
(C) to meet
(D) meeting

10 Nancy hesitated _____ her boyfriend after they had a huge fight.

(A) call
(B) calling
(C) to call
(D) have called

8 _____ for the exam made her exhausted. She fell asleep as soon as she got home.

(A) Study
(B) Studied
(C) Studying
(D) To study

UNIT 3   to부정사와 동명사의 비교

Error Recognition

● TOSEL 기출문제 변형 수능/내신 출제유형

 틀린 문장 고르기

다음 중 문법적으로 틀린 것을 고르세요.

I love ❶ **shopping** for clothes. It's my favorite thing ❷ **to do** . I often go shopping with friends, but if they're busy I will go alone. Yesterday, I bought too many things. Today I will return my new jacket. It's too short for me. I don't usually buy expensive items. I prefer ❸ **to find** bargains. If it's not cheap enough I decide ❹ **not buying** it! Sometimes it's hard ❺ **to find** things that fit well because I'm very tall. Skirts and pants are never long enough. My friend Carrie has the opposite problem. She's very short so everything she buys is too long.

 고쳐쓰기

틀린 문장을 쓰고 올바르게 고치세요.

 _____

 틀린 문장 고르기

다음 중 문법적으로 틀린 것을 고르세요.

> When I grow up I want ❶ to be an actor. My mother said she wants me to be a doctor, but I love acting! I remember ❷ to take a drama class at my school. We put on plays for the other students. Sometimes parents came and watched too. I love ❸ being on stage. I think when I'm older I'd rather act in movies than plays. People who act in movies usually ❹ make more money. I think it would be fun ❺ to be rich.

 고쳐쓰기

틀린 문장을 쓰고 올바르게 고치세요.

  ➜ _____

Unit Review

✏️ 배운 내용 스스로 정리해보기

❶ 의미와 관련한 차이

to부정사는 ❶ 구체적인 것, ❷ [   ], ❸ 가정적인 것을 의미하고,

동명사는 ❶ 일반적인 것, ❷ [   ], ❸ 사실적인 것을 의미한다.

예시문장 써보기

❶ to부정사가 의미하는 [   ] ➡ _____

❷ 동명사가 의미하는 [   ] ➡ _____

❷ to부정사 · 동명사만을 취하는 동사

❶ [   ] 만을 취하는 동사는 ask, decide, want, expect 등이 있고,

❷ [   ] 만을 취하는 동사는 understand, admit, finish, avoid 등이 있다.

예시문장 써보기

❶ [   ] 을(를) 목적 보어로 취하는 expect

➡ _____

❷ [   ] 을(를) 목적어로 취하는 admit

➡ _____

UNIT 04

—

의미상 주어

쓰임

to 부정사의 의미상 주어

❶ for + 목적격

It is necessary **for him to** stay calm.

❷ of + 목적격

It is kind **of you to** help me. 사람의 성격

동명사의 의미상 주어

❶ 소유격을 쓰는 경우: 의미상 주어가 무생물이 아닌 인칭 대명사, 무생물이 아닌 명사일 때

Her be**ing** wise is well known. 무생물이 아닌 인칭대명사

❷ 소유격을 쓰지 않는 경우: 의미상 주어가 무생물일 때

He had a hope <u>of</u> **the train** be**ing** late.

① to부정사의 의미상 주어

❶ 'for+목적격'을 쓰는 경우

She stepped aside <u>for the puppy</u> to **pass**.
부사적 용법

It is natural <u>for her</u> to **be** proud of herself. 'It~ for~ to' 구문
명사적 용법

It is time <u>for you</u> to **go** to bed. 'It~ for~ to' 구문
형용사적 용법

❷ 'of+목적격'을 쓰는 경우

It is thoughtful <u>of you</u> to **call** her. 사람을 주어로 했을 때 의미가 통하는 형용사

It is cruel <u>of you</u> to **hit** the bird. 사람의 성격

② 동명사의 의미상 주어

❶ 소유격을 쓰는 경우

I don't like <u>his</u> **blam**ing others.
무생물이 아닌 인칭대명사

He doesn't like <u>his daughter's</u> **go**ing to the party.
무생물이 아닌 명사

= He doesn't like <u>his daughter</u> **go**ing to the party.
무생물이 아닌 명사는 목적격으로도 사용 가능

❷ 소유격을 쓰지 않는 경우

They were glad of <u>the war</u> **be**ing over.
무생물

There is a hope of <u>her health</u> **improv**ing.
무생물(추상명사)

NOTE ✎

Activity

밑줄 친 부분에 주의해서 문장을 해석해보세요.

1 It is so kind <u>of her</u> to help me finish the project.

➡

2 Do you mind <u>my</u> closing the window?

➡

3 It is stupid <u>of him</u> to lend such money to her.

➡

4 I like <u>her</u> coming here.

➡

5 They insisted on <u>my</u> participating in the game.

➡

6 I am proud <u>of my granddaughter's</u> being a doctor.

➡

7 It is necessary <u>for me</u> to see a professor.

➡

8 There's no evidence <u>of their</u> having invented this language.

➡

9 It is difficult <u>for her</u> to finish the homework.

➡

10 I complained <u>of the subway</u> being too crowded.

➡

Exercise

 Exercise 1

괄호에서 알맞은 것을 모두 고르세요.

❶ It is impossible   of him / for him   to study such a difficult subject.

❷ It was careless   of her / for her   not to bring her assignment to school.

❸ It is hard   for him / of him   to have a part time job and go to school.

❹ Jacob insisted on   I / my   staying with his daughter.

❺ My mother enjoys   Ø / her   wearing a scarf.

 Exercise 2

밑줄 친 부분이 틀리다면 바르게 고쳐 보세요. (맞는 문장일 수 있음)

❶ The assignment was easy **to me** to complete.
→

❷ They decided to move **for them** to another country next year.
→

❸ We are proud **of your** being a lawyer.
→

❹ It is cruel **to you** to treat your dog like that.
→

 Exercise 3

어법에 맞게 괄호 안을 채워넣으세요.

① 나는 그가 나를 목장에 데려갔던 것을 기억했다. (he)

I remembered _____ bringing me to the ranch.

② 그녀의 할머니께서는 그녀가 1등을 할 것이라고 확신하신다. (she)

Her grandmother is sure of _____ winning the first prize.

③ 그가 그 빌딩을 설계하는 것은 어려운 일이었다. (he)

It was difficult _____ to design the building.

④ 그가 충치를 예방하기 위해 이를 닦는 것은 반드시 필요하다. (he)

It is necessary _____ to brush his teeth to prevent further cavities.

⑤ 네가 이 문제를 풀어내다니 너는 매우 영리하구나. (you)

It is very clever _____ to solve this problem.

Sentence Completion

1 A : What is the price _____ to enter the museum?

  B : It will be $20 each.

(A) kids

(B) kids'

(C) of kids

(D) for kids

4 A : _____ being here is still unbelievable.

  B : Me too.

(A) Your

(B) Yours

(C) You are

(D) Yourself

2 A : Did you hear that Sally saved a baby?

  B : Yes. It was very brave _____ her to save someone's life.

(A) to

(B) by

(C) of

(D) for

5 A : Speaking of _____ moving to Chicago, he bought a house there.

  B : Oh, really?

(A) he

(B) his

(C) he's

(D) himself

3 A : Do you mind _____ sitting next to you?

  B : Yes, actually this seat is taken.

(A) I

(B) my

(C) mine

(D) myself

6 It can be very dangerous ▢▢▢▢ children to go outside without their parents.

(A) to
(B) of
(C) by
(D) for

9 My parents approved of ▢▢▢▢ studying abroad.

(A) I
(B) my
(C) mine
(D) myself

7 It was rude ▢▢▢▢ Helen to storm out of the meeting.

(A) to
(B) of
(C) for
(D) with

10 We were so pleased with ▢▢▢▢ being finished.

(A) the exam
(B) the exam's
(C) the exam is
(D) the exam was

8 I have been waiting so long ▢▢▢▢ their concert to be held.

(A) to
(B) of
(C) for
(D) with

Error Recognition

● TOSEL 기출문제 변형 수능/내신 출제유형

 틀린 문장 고르기

다음 중 문법적으로 틀린 것을 고르세요.

Shrek is a ❶ **very** popular animated film that came out in the year 2001. The main characters in the movie are Shrek, Princess Fiona, ❷ **and** Donkey. Shrek is a green ogre who has a kind heart. Fiona is a beautiful princess who Shrek must save. Donkey is Shrek's funny, helpful friend. All three characters learn something ❸ **new** about themselves as they all work together to stop the evil Lord Farquaad. ❹ **The movie's** being popular gave them a chance ❺ **to make** two more movies.

 고쳐쓰기

틀린 문장을 쓰고 올바르게 고치세요.

_____

 틀린 문장 고르기

다음 중 문법적으로 틀린 것을 고르세요.

Joe does all the grocery shopping for his family. He enjoys ❶ going to the supermarket. It usually takes two hours ❷ of him to get all his groceries. He makes sure he ❸ is getting only the freshest fruit and vegetables. Joe buys the same food every week unless there's a sale. Last week there was a sale on fish, so he bought one for ❹ himself and one for his wife. She loved it. He fried it in a pan with lemon and butter. This week Joe doesn't see any good sales. He buys fruits and vegetables and ❺ goes home.

 고쳐쓰기

틀린 문장을 쓰고 올바르게 고치세요.

  ➔ _____

UNIT 4 의미상 주어

✎ 배운 내용 스스로 정리해보기

❶ to부정사의 의미상 주어

to 부정사의 의미상 주어는 ❶ [   ] 을(를) 쓰는 경우와

❷ [   ] 을(를) 쓰는 경우로 나누어진다.

예시문장 써보기

❶ to부정사의 부사적 용법 앞의 [   ]

→ _____

❷ 사람의 성격을 나타내는 형용사 뒤의 [   ]

→ _____

❷ 동명사의 의미상 주어

동명사의 의미상 주어는 ❶ [   ] 와(과)

❷ [   ] (으)로 나누어진다.

예시문장 써보기

❶ [   ] (무생물이 아닌 명사)

→ _____

❷ [   ] (무생물)

→ _____

TOSEL 실전문제 ⑤

PART 6. Sentence Completion

DIRECTIONS: In this portion of the test, you will be given 10 incomplete sentences. From the choices provided, choose the word or words that correctly complete the sentence. Then, fill in the corresponding space on your answer sheet.

1. A: I'm really hungry.
    B: I know the way _____ chicken soup. I'll make it for you.

    (A) make
    (B) made
    (C) to make
    (D) was making

4. A: Susan, how have you been?
    B: Good, thanks. Actually, I decided _____ abroad.

    (A) move
    (B) moving
    (C) to move
    (D) having been moved

2. A: Amy's birthday is coming. What should we prepare?
    B: Well, I already booked a restaurant _____ her birthday.

    (A) celebrate
    (B) to celebrate
    (C) is celebrating
    (D) have celebrated

5. A: Mr. Collins looks upset. Why?
    B: He doesn't like _____ going to the party, but she went there.

    (A) she
    (B) hers
    (C) of her
    (D) his daughter's

3. A: I feel exhausted every day.
    B: How about jogging with me? I enjoy _____ every morning.

    (A) jog
    (B) jogged
    (C) will jog
    (D) jogging

6. Bob failed to qualify. I was unhappy _____ the news.

   (A) hear
   (B) heard
   (C) to hear
   (D) be hearing

9. The main culprit admitted _____ the murder. He will be punished by the law.

   (A) commit
   (B) to commit
   (C) committing
   (D) is committing

7. Amanda was accused of a strange rumor three years ago. But it was proved _____ false.

   (A) be
   (B) to be
   (C) being
   (D) having been

10. It was careless _____ you to mention the accident. She is still suffering from the trauma.

   (A) in
   (B) of
   (C) by
   (D) for

8. I really love _____, but since the virus is going around the entire world, I cannot travel.

   (A) traveling
   (B) is traveling
   (C) have traveled
   (D) being traveling

Error Recognition

1. 다음 중 문법적으로 틀린 것을 골라 고치세요.

● TOSEL 기출문제 변형 수능/내신 출제유형

1

In the 19th century, many people in America moved West. They wanted **①** **exploring** new, wild areas without big cities. Many people started their journey from St. Louis, so they called it the Gateway City. In 1963, St. Louis built the Gateway Arch **②** **to remember** that time. Today, you can go to the top of the Arch and look at the city. From the windows at the top, you can see the longest river in America. **③** **Imagine** how those early explorers felt looking at the same scene!

 _____

2. 다음 밑줄 친 부분을 바르게 고치세요.

● TOSEL 기출문제 변형 수능/내신 출제유형

2

In South America, you might see people **to play** an unusual instrument. When they first put it to their mouth, maybe it will look like they are eating a potato. It is not a potato, though. It is a musical instrument called an ocarina. There is one hole at the top to blow into, and many smaller holes for your fingers. One reason ocarinas are popular is that they are easy to play. To change the sound, cover some holes with your fingers. It's that simple!

 → _____

CHAPTER 06

UNIT 01

비교급과 최상급의 규칙 변화

> **생김새**
>
> ❶ **비교급:** '원급 + -er' 또는 'more + 원급'
>
> He is **tall**<u>er</u> than me.
>
> ❷ **비교급의 비교:** '비교급+than...'
>
> He is **small**<u>er</u> **than** me.
>
> ---
>
> ❶ **최상급:** 'the + 원급 + -est' 또는 'the + most + 원급'
>
> He is **the tall**<u>est</u> student in the school.
>
> ❷ **최상급의 비교:** '최상급 + of[in]...'
>
> He is **the tall**<u>est</u> **of** all the students.

1 비교급의 규칙 변화

❶ 원급에 -er을 붙이는 경우

Noah is **young**er **than** her. 단음절어의 경우

Come **close**r. -e로 끝나는 경우

Daegu is **hot**ter **than** Seoul. 단모음+단자음의 경우

It is **eas**ier to walk **than** to run. 자음+y의 경우

❷ 원급 앞에 more를 붙이는 경우

This pen is more **useful than** that one. 2음절어

His homework is more **difficult than** mine. 3음절어 이상

2 최상급의 규칙 변화

❶ 원급에 -est를 붙이는 경우

Noah is **the young**est of us. 단음절어의 경우

She was **the close**st person to me. -e로 끝나는 경우

Daegu is **the hot**test city in Korea. 단모음+단자음의 경우

That is **the eas**iest way to go home. 자음+y의 경우

❷ 원급 앞에 most를 붙이는 경우

This is **the most useful** pen I have ever used. 2음절어

Poverty is **the most difficult** problem we must solve. 3음절어 이상

Activity

주어진 단어를 비교급 또는 최상급으로 바꿔보세요.

---

1 useful (비교급)   (   )

2 hot (최상급)   (   )

3 easy (최상급)   (   )

4 difficult (비교급)   (   )

5 expensive (최상급)   (   )

6 close (비교급)   (   )

7 young (비교급)   (   )

8 cheap (최상급)   (   )

9 warm (비교급)   (   )

10 comfortable (최상급)   (   )

Exercise

 ## Exercise 1

둘 중 맞는 단어를 고르세요.

1 This puzzle is **more complex / complexer** than yours.

2 She is **the most famous / the famousest** person among my friends.

3 I think writing is **the easiest / the easyest** of all activities.

4 A squirrel is **more small / smaller** than a tiger.

5 Cindy is **more smart / smarter** than Rachel.

 ## Exercise 2

주어진 단어를 이용하여 괄호 안을 비교급 또는 최상급으로 바꾸어보세요.

1 A turtle is _____ than a rabbit. (slow)

2 This dress is _____ than the skirt. (expensive)

3 I think she was _____ among all guests. (pretty)

4 The exam was _____ than I had expected. (difficult)

5 I bet I can run _____ than her. (fast)

다음 문장의 밑줄 친 부분이 틀렸다면 올바르게 고쳐보세요. (맞는 문장일 수도 있음)

❶ I heard that she is **older** than you.

➡

❷ He was **more happy** than me.

➡

❸ This room is the **most big** room in this house.

➡

❹ That is the **most easy** way to go to school.

➡

❺ This new navigation is **usefuler** than the old one.

➡

UNIT 1 비교급과 최상급의 규칙 변화

Sentence Completion

1 A : How was the movie?

  B : It was ▢▢▢▢▢ than the one we saw last week.

(A) funny

(B) funnier

(C) funniest

(D) more funnier

2 A : This novel is so long.

  B : The second book is ▢▢▢▢▢ than that one.

(A) longer

(B) longest

(C) more long

(D) most long

3 A : That salad looks tasty.

  B : It is actually ▢▢▢▢▢ than I expected.

(A) tasty

(B) tastier

(C) tastiest

(D) as tasty

4 A : What is the ▢▢▢▢▢ food in Korea?

  B : I think it is Kimchi-jjigae.

(A) delicious

(B) deliciouser

(C) more delicious

(D) most delicious

5 A : Who is the ▢▢▢▢▢ girl in your class?

  B : It's Sujin. I heard she is 175cm tall.

(A) taller

(B) tallest

(C) more tall

(D) most tall

6 The Hermitage is ⬚⬚⬚⬚⬚⬚ than the Louvre in Paris.

(A) small

(B) smaller

(C) as small

(D) more small

7 A pigeon delivers a message ⬚⬚⬚⬚⬚⬚ than the Internet.

(A) slower

(B) more slow

(C) most slow

(D) as slow as

8 Playing the alphorn was ⬚⬚⬚⬚⬚⬚ than Marco had expected.

(A) easy

(B) easily

(C) easier

(D) easiest

9 Among the many projects Wangari Maathai did, the Green Belt Movement is ⬚⬚⬚⬚⬚⬚ .

(A) famously

(B) famouser

(C) the famousest

(D) the most famous

10 He says that in opera, music is ⬚⬚⬚⬚⬚⬚ part.

(A) important

(B) the importantest

(C) the most important

(D) the more important

Error Recognition

 틀린 문장 고르기

다음 중 문법적으로 틀린 것을 고르세요.

Mount Everest is ❶ **the taller** mountain in the world. ❷ **It** is 29,028 feet high, or about 5.5 miles above sea level. Mount Everest is part ❸ **of** the Himalayan Mountain range and is located between the countries of Tibet and Nepal. It is about 60 million ❹ **years** old. About 4,000 people have tried to climb Mount Everest, ❺ **but** only 660 have made it to the top.

 고쳐쓰기

틀린 문장을 쓰고 올바르게 고치세요.

➡ _____

 ## 틀린 문장 고르기

다음 중 문법적으로 틀린 것을 고르세요.

I love big cities. I ❶ **grew up** in the country. The country is beautiful, but I like cities ❷ **because** they're big and busy. I love the noise ❸ **from** all the cars and people. I also love all the different restaurants and theaters. In the country, I could walk for a long time and not see another person. In the city, there are people everywhere. In the country, you need ❹ **to walk** everywhere or own a car. In the city, I just get on the subway. It's ❺ **more cheap** than a car and faster than walking.

 ## 고쳐쓰기

틀린 문장을 쓰고 올바르게 고치세요.

✏️ 배운 내용 스스로 정리해보기

① 비교급의 규칙 변화

단음절어의 경우, ❶ [   ] (으)로 끝나는 경우, '단모음+단자음'의 경우, ❷ [   ] 의 경우 원급에 -er을 붙이고, ❸ [   ], 3음절어 이상의 경우에 원급 앞에 more를 붙인다.

예시문장 써보기

❶ [   ] (으)로 끝나는 경우 ➡ _____

❷ [   ] 의 경우 ➡ _____

❸ [   ] ➡ _____

② 최상급의 규칙 변화

단음절어의 경우, -e(으)로 끝나는 경우, '단모음+단자음'의 경우, ❶ [   ] 의 경우 원급에 -est를 붙이고, ❷ [   ], ❸ [   ] 의 경우에 원급 앞에 most를 붙인다.

예시문장 써보기

❶ [   ] 의 경우 ➡ _____

❷ [   ] ➡ _____

❸ [   ] 의 경우 ➡ _____

UNIT 02

비교급과 최상급의 불규칙 변화

생김새	**good**(원급)**-better**(비교급)**-best**(최상급)와 같이 원급, 비교급, 최상급의 형태가 불규칙적으로 변함
	ex) This idea is <u>good</u>.
	→ This idea is <u>better</u> than the previous idea.
	→ This idea is <u>the best</u> of all of the ideas.

<table>
<tr><td rowspan="5">종류</td>
<td colspan="3">
<table>
<thead>
<tr><th>원급</th><th>비교급</th><th>최상급</th></tr>
</thead>
<tbody>
<tr><td>good
well</td><td>better</td><td>best</td></tr>
<tr><td>bad
ill</td><td>worse</td><td>worst</td></tr>
<tr><td>many
much</td><td>more</td><td>most</td></tr>
<tr><td>little</td><td>less</td><td>least</td></tr>
</tbody>
</table>
</td></tr>
</table>

ex) I have <u>bad</u> eyesight.

→ I have <u>worse</u> eyesight than him.

→ I have <u>the worst</u> eyesight in the class.

비교급과 최상급의 불규칙 변화

원급	비교급	최상급
good well	better	best
bad	worse	worst
many much	more	most
old	older elder	oldest eldest
late	later latter	latest (시간) last (순서)
far	farther further	farthest (거리) furthest (거리,정도)
little	less	least
up	upper	up(per) most
in	inner	in(ner) most

NOTE 🖉

TIP **elder, eldest**

● elder, eldest는 사람에 관한 이야기를 할 때 사용한다.

* 특히, 가족 또는 사회 관계 내에서 비교를 할 때 사용한다.

Her voice is good.

➜ Her voice is better (than his).

➜ Her voice is the best.

Jane is old.

➜ Jane is older (than me).

➜ Jane is the oldest.

✎ Activity

주어진 단어를 비교급 또는 최상급으로 바꿔보세요.

❶ good (비교급)   (   )

❷ much (최상급)   (   )

❸ late (최상급, 순서)   (   )

❹ little (비교급)   (   )

❺ up (최상급)   (   )

❻ little (최상급)   (   )

❼ bad (비교급)   (   )

❽ in (최상급)   (   )

❾ well (최상급)   (   )

❿ far (최상급, 거리/정도)   (   )

UNIT 2 비교급과 최상급의 불규칙 변화

Exercise

 ## Exercise 1

둘 중 맞는 단어를 고르세요.

❶ My voice is   **better / more good**   than hers.

❷ It was the   **worst / most bad**   score that I ever got.

❸ We all believe that he could jump   **farther / more far**   .

❹ Did you hear the   **last / latest**   news about the epidemic?

❺ The doctor advised me to eat   **more little / less**   food.

 ## Exercise 2

주어진 단어를 이용하여 괄호 안을 비교급 또는 최상급으로 바꾸어보세요.

❶ She earns   money than her husband. (little)

❷ His   painting is well-known for its ingenuity. (late, 시간)

❸ I want to study   about the cognition ability of animals. (far, 정도)

❹ We think what he suggested is the   solution for the problem. (good)

❺   than 40 students participated in the survey. (many)

✏ Exercise 3

다음 문장의 밑줄 친 부분이 틀렸다면 올바르게 고쳐보세요. (맞는 문장일 수도 있음)

① Why don't we discuss it **<u>further</u>?**

➡

② It was the **<u>most little</u>** important part of this chapter.

➡

③ I feel much **<u>more good</u>** than yesterday thanks to the pill.

➡

④ He arrived at the station **<u>latter</u>** than had predicted.

➡

⑤ His memory is **<u>more bad</u>** than yours.

➡

Sentence Completion

1 A : Gosh, the meeting with my boss was
       the ▢▢▢▢▢
    B : What happened?

(A) bad
(B) worst
(C) baddest
(D) most bad

2 A : Did you read the ▢▢▢▢▢
       chapter of this book?
    B : Yes, it was so good.

(A) last
(B) later
(C) latter
(D) latest

3 A : What is ▢▢▢▢▢ way to get
       into that program?
    B : Study extra hard and do lots of
       volunteer work.

(A) good
(B) the best
(C) the most good
(D) the most better

4 A : Did you hear the news?
       The ▢▢▢▢▢ story of our office
       was set on fire yesterday!
    B : Yeah, I heard that nobody was injured.

(A) up
(B) uppest
(C) most up
(D) uppermost

5 A : I love this author.
    B : Me, too. I think her ▢▢▢▢▢
       work is <A Room of One's Own>.

(A) good
(B) best
(C) better
(D) most good

6 Many people thought the original novel was _____ than the film.

(A) good
(B) well
(C) better
(D) more good

9 Some neurons that form the memory move _____ into the brain.

(A) far
(B) further
(C) farthest
(D) furthest

7 She thinks safety matters _____ than water and food.

(A) many
(B) much
(C) most
(D) more

10 Beam bridges are the _____ stable type of bridge.

(A) little
(B) less
(C) least
(D) most little

8 This town is where the world's _____ person lives.

(A) older
(B) elder
(C) oldest
(D) more old

UNIT 2   비교급과 최상급의 불규칙 변화

Error Recognition

● TOSEL 기출문제 변형 수능/내신 출제유형

 ## 틀린 문장 고르기

다음 중 문법적으로 틀린 것을 고르세요.

My vacation was fun. I saw many new things. I got **①** **to see** some big mountains. My father wanted me to ski on the mountain but I said "no way!" My father is a much **②** **more good** skier than me. I'd rather go swimming or shopping. My mother and I went **③** **shopping** in some neat shops. In one shop they were making homemade fudge. My mother and I watched them **④** **make** it, then we bought enough for the whole family. It was **⑤** **sweet and delicious** !

 ## 고쳐쓰기

틀린 문장을 쓰고 올바르게 고치세요.

_____

✏️ 틀린 문장 고르기

다음 중 문법적으로 틀린 것을 고르세요.

> The black bear is usually 4 to 7 feet from nose **①** **to** tail, and two to three feet high. It has small eyes, rounded ears, a long snout, a large body, a short tail, and **②** **shaggy** hair. It differs from grizzly bears in **③** **being** smaller. It has a smaller shoulder hump, a furred rearfoot, smaller claws that are **④** **many** tightly curved, and longer, **⑤** **smoother** ears.

✏️ 고쳐쓰기

틀린 문장을 쓰고 올바르게 고치세요.

➡️ _____

Unit Review

① 비교급과 최상급의 불규칙 변화

원급	비교급	최상급
good well	better	best
bad	①	worst
many much	more	most
old	older elder	oldest eldest
late	later latter	② ③
far	④ further	farthest (거리) furthest (거리,정도)
little	less	⑤
up	upper	up(per) most
in	inner	in(ner) most

예시문장 써보기

①   → _____

②   → _____

③   → _____

④   → _____

⑤   → _____

UNIT 03

원급의 비교

❶ **동등비교**: 'as+원급+as'

ex) My son is **as wise as** my wife.

❷ **열등비교**: 'not as[so]+원급+as' 또는

'less+원급+than'

ex) My son is **not as[so]** wise **as** my wife.

= My son is **less wise than** my wife.

❷ **배수비교**: '배수사+as+원급+as' 또는

'배수사+the 명사+of'

ex) The cake is **twice as large as** the pie.

ex) The cake is **twice the size of** the pie.

1 동등비교

' as + 원급 + as '

Mary is <u>as tall as</u> Tom.

Mary is <u>as tall</u> **a student** <u>as</u> Tom.

2 열등비교

' not + so + 원급 + as '

Mary is <u>not so tall as</u> Tom.
= Mary is **less** tall **than** Tom.

She is <u>not so happy nor so unhappy as</u> we imagine.

3 배수비교

기본 형태 : ' 배수사 (twice / half, three times, …) **+ as + 원급 + as '**

This is **two times** <u>as large as</u> that.
= This is **two times larg**er than that.
= This is **two times** <u>the size of</u> that.

❶ 명사 표현이 있는 경우

Your house is **three** <u>times the size of</u> mine.

I have **three** <u>times as many books as</u> you.

❷ 원급을 이용한 어구

This is **half** <u>as large as</u> that.

This is **twice** <u>as large as</u> that.
= This is <u>as large again as</u> that.

NOTE ✎

Activity

주어진 문장의 비교 형태를 파악하고, 해석해보세요.

❶ My daughter is as wise as my husband.   (동등비교 / 열등비교)

❷ My son is not so wise as my wife.   (동등비교 / 열등비교)

❸ My son is less wise than my wife.   (동등비교 / 열등비교)

❹ The banana is twice as large as the apple.   (동등비교 / 배수비교)

❺ The banana is two times larger than the apple.   (동등비교 / 배수비교)

❻ I have five times as much work as they have.   (열등비교 / 배수비교)

❼ The ocean is three times the depth of the river.   (동등비교 / 배수비교)

❽ Jane is not so kind as Rosa.   (동등비교 / 열등비교)

❾ Jacob is as handsome as Leonardo.   (동등비교 / 열등비교)

❿ Sue has twice as many books as Richard.   (동등비교 / 배수비교)

Exercise

Exercise 1

주어진 단어를 이용하여 괄호 안을 채워보세요.

---

❶ 그녀는 나만큼이나 프랑스어를 유창하게 한다. (fluently)

She speaks French ▢▢▢▢▢▢ me.

❷ 나는 Amy 만큼 똑똑하지 않아서 공부를 열심히 해야한다. (smart)

I'm not ▢▢▢▢▢ Amy, so I have to study hard.

❸ Tom의 말에 따르면 그녀는 우리가 상상하는 것 만큼 부유하지는 않다. (rich)

She is not ▢▢▢▢ we imagine according to what Tom said.

❹ 이 책은 저 책보다 다섯 배 더 두껍다. (five times, thick)

This book is ▢▢▢▢▢▢▢ that book.

❺ Kate는 Rosa만큼 키가 큰 학생이다. (tall, student)

Kate is ▢▢▢▢▢ Rosa.

Exercise 2

문법 상 알맞은 단어를 골라보세요.

---

❶ You are as tall as   **him / he**   .

❷ Maybe this book is   **as expensive / more expensive**   as an iPad.

❸ It wasn't   **as so interesting / so interesting**   as the one I watched yesterday.

❹ The population here is one-fourth as   **large / largely**   as that of your state.

❺ I have three times   **many clothes / as many clothes**   as you have.

Exercise 3

주어진 단어를 문법에 맞게 빈칸을 올바른 문장으로 배열해보세요.

❶ This laptop is _____ that one.
   (times/heavier/three/than)

❷ Hydrogen fuels are _____ conventional fossil fuels.
   (as/times/as/efficient/five)

❸ This room is _____ that room beside the kitchen.
   (large/as/half/as)

❹ My dog became almost _____ of me.
   (size/two/the/times)

❺ The boy is _____ my daughter.
   (so/not/as/polite)

UNIT 3 원급의 비교

Sentence Completion

❶ A : I became as ▨▨▨▨▨ as you
　　are.

　B : Wow, good for you!

　(A) tall
　(B) taller
　(C) tallest
　(D) the tall

❷ A : Oh, no! My English score is not so
　　▨▨▨▨▨ as I expected.

　B : It's okay. You'll do better next time.

　(A) well
　(B) best
　(C) good
　(D) better

❸ A : I think Brad is not ▨▨▨▨▨ as
　　Tom.

　B : What? I can't agree with you.

　(A) so handsome
　(B) so handsomer
　(C) so more handsome
　(D) so most handsome

❹ A : This book is twice as ▨▨▨▨▨
　　as that textbook. How can I carry
　　this?

　B : Let me give you a hand.

　(A) heavy
　(B) heavier
　(C) heaviest
　(D) so heavy

❺ A : This wall is twice ▨▨▨▨▨ that
　　building.

　B : Wow, that's amazing.

　(A) as old as
　(B) as older as
　(C) as young as
　(D) as younger as

6 It is a mystery how an artist could get so much detail into works of art as as a Persian miniature.

(A) tiny

(B) tinier

(C) more tiny

(D) most tiny

9 This skyscraper is three times my house.

(A) high

(B) highly

(C) more high

(D) as high as

7 In musicals, the details of the lyrics are not those of the story.

(A) so important

(B) as important

(C) so important as

(D) as more important

10 My grandmother is four times than I am.

(A) old

(B) older

(C) as older as

(D) as oldly as

8 Babies do not need oxygen as adults.

(A) so much

(B) so more

(C) many more

(D) much more

Error Recognition

 틀린 문장 고르기

다음 중 문법적으로 틀린 것을 고르세요.

Last Wednesday was such a beautiful day. The sun was shining and the birds ❶ **were singing** . There was a soft wind blowing from the west. It was warm enough that I didn't need a jacket. It seemed like a beautiful day ❷ **to ride** my bike in the park. I ❸ **grabbed** a snack, and my sunglasses. I was ready for a bike ride! Just as I arrived at the park, I noticed dark grey clouds in the sky. The sky was not as ❹ **more beautiful** as in the morning. There was a loud bang followed by lightning. The rain started ❺ **to pour down** . I guess it wasn't such a good day for a bike ride after all.

 고쳐쓰기

틀린 문장을 쓰고 올바르게 고치세요.

 → _____

✏️ 틀린 문장 고르기

다음 중 문법적으로 틀린 것을 고르세요.

My dog Alex loves **①** **to bark** . I think it's his favorite activity. I know Alex loves **②** **me** a lot. He runs around in circles and cries **③** **when** I leave the house for school. My mom and dad both work so I think he gets lonely being home by himself all day. But I think my love for Alex is two times **④** **large** than his. It means that I'd be lonely too. Sometimes I leave the TV on in the living room. I think if he hears the people talking on TV it might make him less lonely. **⑤** **As soon as** I come home, I always give him a treat so he knows I'm happy to see him too.

✏️ 고쳐쓰기

틀린 문장을 쓰고 올바르게 고치세요.

➡️ _____

✏️ 배운 내용 스스로 정리해보기

❶ 동등비교

동등비교의 형태는 ❶ [   ] (이)다.

예시문장 써보기

❶ [   ] → _____

❷ 열등비교

열등비교의 형태는 ❶ [   ] 또는 ❷ [   ] (이)다.

예시문장 써보기

❶ [   ] → _____

❷ [   ] → _____

❸ 배수비교

배수비교의 형태는 ❶ [   ] (이)다.

이러한 형태는 ❷ [   ] (으)로 전환될 수 있다.

예시문장 써보기

❶ [   ] (원급 big 사용)

→ _____

❷ [   ] (명사 size 사용)

→ _____

UNIT 04

최상급의 비교

생김새

❶ 'the + 최상급 + of all (the)

+ 복수명사 [of+복수대명사]'

ex) This is **the most expensive of** all (the) books.

ex) He is **the strongest of** all **of** them.

❷ 'the + 최상급 + in (the) + 장소'

ex) This is **the most expensive** book **in** this store.

❸ 'the + 최상급 + 명사 + (that) ~ever [can]'

ex) She is **the most honest** person ever lived.

ex) This is **the most expensive** book you could find.

1 최상급의 형태

NOTE 🖉

> **❶ the + 최상급 + of all(the) + 복수명사 [of + 복수대명사]**
>
> He is **the tall**est of all (the) students.
>
> He is **the tall**est of us.

> **❷ the + 최상급 + in (the) + 장소**
>
> He is **the tall**est in his class.

> **❸ the + 최상급 + 명사 + (that) ~ever [can]**
>
> He is **the wis**est man (that) ever lived.
>
> This is **the cheap**est car (that) you could find.

2 the를 붙이지 않는 최상급

> **❶ 동일인이나 동일물의 성질, 상태의 비교**
>
> This lake is **deep**est at this point.

> **❷ 서술적으로 쓰인 최상급**
>
> He was **happi**est when he was young.

> **❸ 부사의 최상급**
>
> He ran **fast**est.

> **❹ 소유격으로 대체된 경우**
>
> It is his **great**est pleasure to meet her.

> **❺ '대부분의' 뜻일 때**
>
> Most of the lakes in America are beautiful.

Activity

보기를 참고하여 주어진 단어를 이용해 최상급 문장으로 만들어보세요.

> **보기** **She, wise , students, class**
>
> ➡ She is the wisest of all students.
> ➡ She is the wisest in her class.

① He, tall, students, class

➡

➡

② This book, expensive, books, shelf

➡

➡

③ The baby, cute, babies, kindergarten

➡

➡

④ The statue, high, artifacts, world

➡

➡

⑤ The Pacific, wide, oceans, world

➡

➡

Exercise

 ## Exercise 1

주어진 단어를 이용하여 괄호 안을 채워보세요.

① 그는 그의 반에서 가장 똑똑하다. (smart)

He is _____ in his class.

② 이것은 네가 찾을 수 있는 가방 중 가장 싼 것이다. (cheap)

This is _____ bag that you could ever find.

③ 이 산은 이 높이에서 가장 가파르다. (steep)

This mountain is _____ at this height.

④ 그녀는 고등학교에 다닐 때 가장 불행했다. (unhappy)

She was _____ when she was in high school.

⑤ 그녀는 우리 중에서 가장 부유해서 우리에게 항상 많은 선물들을 사준다. (rich)

She is _____ of us, so she always buys us many gifts.

 ## Exercise 2

문법상 알맞은 단어를 골라보세요.

① The river is   the deepest / deepest   at this point.

②   The most / Most   people subscribe to this newspaper.

③ It is my   the greatest / greatest   pleasure to be invited here at this party.

④ Summer is   hottest/ the hottest   .

⑤ She swam   the fastest / fastest   of all athletes.

Exercise 3

다음 문장의 밑줄 친 부분이 틀렸다면 올바르게 고쳐보세요. (맞는 문장일 수도 있음)

① This is **most expensive** car you could ever find.

➡

② It was **best** moment throughout the show.

➡

③ She has **the longest** hair among us.

➡

④ It was my **the biggest** pleasure to go out with her.

➡

⑤ **The most** of us participated in the survey.

➡

UNIT 4 최상급의 비교

Sentence Completion

1 A : What's the _____ thing you've ever eaten?

B : Thai chili pepper.

(A) spicy
(B) spiciest
(C) spiciness
(D) most spicy

2 A : What do you think is the _____ love of all?

B : I think it is parents' love for their children.

(A) great
(B) greater
(C) greatest
(D) most great

3 A : What is the sticker on your hand?

B : I ran _____ of all my classmates so my P.E. teacher gave it to me.

(A) fast
(B) faster
(C) fastest
(D) the fastest

4 A : Which prize would you be _____ to win?

B : I think it would be the Fields Medal.

(A) pride
(B) proudest
(C) the proudest
(D) the most proud

5 A : _____ people don't like to try unfamiliar things. How about you?

B : I love to try new things.

(A) Most
(B) The more
(C) The most
(D) The many

6 Nicola Tesla and Thomas Edison were the _____ rivals in the scientific world of electricity.

(A) big
(B) bigger
(C) biggest
(D) most big

9 He taught her about his _____ invention: the difference engine.

(A) newer
(B) newest
(C) more new
(D) most new

7 The Great Green Wall will be the world's _____ living structure ever built when it is finished.

(A) larger
(B) largest
(C) more large
(D) most large

10 _____ of all was when Fred Lorz was declared the winner.

(A) Strange
(B) Stranger
(C) Strangest
(D) The strangest

8 The oldest writer _____ Venezuela passed away last year.

(A) in
(B) of
(C) with
(D) within

UNIT 4 최상급과 비교

Error Recognition

 틀린 문장 고르기

다음 중 문법적으로 틀린 것을 고르세요.

Family is very important to Katie. She has **①** the bigger family I've ever seen. She has two younger sisters and an older brother. Her brother taught **②** her how to play basketball. He's really good. He's on his high school basketball team. In the morning she helps her younger sisters **③** pick what to wear. They both love **④** to dress up so Katie usually lets them wear a dress, or a skirt and blouse. Katie would rather wear jeans and a t-shirt. She thinks it's **⑤** more comfortable . Sometimes Katie's mom asks her to wear a dress. The last time she wore a dress was for school pictures.

 고쳐쓰기

틀린 문장을 쓰고 올바르게 고치세요.

→ _____

 ## 틀린 문장 고르기

다음 중 문법적으로 틀린 것을 고르세요.

Basketball is an **①** **exciting** sport. **②** **The most** people who play basketball are tall. The taller the player, the closer they are to the net. **③** **To play** basketball, it's important **④** **to be** in good shape. Players must run repeatedly and quickly. Basketball **⑤** **was invented** by a man named James Naismith. During the first basketball game, peach baskets were used instead of nets.

 ## 고쳐쓰기

틀린 문장을 쓰고 올바르게 고치세요.

 ➜ _____

Unit Review

✏️ 배운 내용 스스로 정리해보기

① 최상급의 형태

최상급의 형태는 ① 'the + 최상급 +   ',

② 'the + 최상급 +   ', ③ 'the + 최상급 +   ' (이)다.

예시문장 써보기

① 'the + 최상급 +

→ _____

② 'the + 최상급 +

→ _____

③ 'the + 최상급 +

→ _____

② the를 붙이지 않는 최상급

the를 붙이지 않는 최상급이 쓰이는 경우는 ① 동일인이나 동일물의 성질·상태의 비교,

②   , ③ 소유격으로 대체된 경우, ④ 부사의 최상급인 경우,

⑤   이다.

예시문장 써보기

① 동일인이나 동일물의 성질·상태의 비교

→ _____

②

→ _____

TOSEL 실전문제 ❻

PART 6. Sentence Completion

DIRECTIONS: In this portion of the test, you will be given 10 incomplete sentences. From the choices provided, choose the word or words that correctly complete the sentence. Then, fill in the corresponding space on your answer sheet.

1. A: This novel is so long.
    B: The second book is _____ than that one.

    (A) longer
    (B) longest
    (C) more long
    (D) most long

2. A: That salad looks tasty.
    B: It is actually _____ than I expected.

    (A) tasty
    (B) tasitier
    (C) tastiest
    (D) more tasty

3. A: This concert is much _____ than the one I saw last year.
    B: I don't think so. The stage set was so beautiful.

    (A) bad
    (B) worse
    (C) more bad
    (D) most badest

4. A: Did Jane get a better score than Amy? She studied really hard.
    B: No, Amy got a better score. Jane is _____ as Amy.

    (A) clever
    (B) as clever
    (C) so clever
    (D) not so clever

5. A: This river seems shallow, doesn't it?
    B: Watch out! This river is _____ at this point.

    (A) deepest
    (B) the deepest
    (C) the most deep
    (D) the most deepest

6. The movie was _____ than the one we saw last week.

(A) funny
(B) funnier
(C) funniest
(D) more funnier

7. It is _____ thing for James to socialize with new people. He is introverted.

(A) the difficulty
(B) the most difficult
(C) the more difficult
(D) the most difficulty

8. We should avoid splurging on things. So she bought _____ expensive skirt.

(A) the least
(B) the most less
(C) the more less
(D) the most least

9. Wow, he dances _____ she does! He must have practiced dancing so hard.

(A) well
(B) better
(C) so well as
(D) as well as

10. Mr. Ranton is known as _____ man that ever lived in this town.

(A) wise
(B) wisest
(C) the wisest
(D) the most wisest

Error Recognition

 1. 다음 중 문법적으로 틀린 것을 골라 고치세요.

● TOSEL 기출문제 변형 수능/내신 출제유형

1

Optical Illusions can trick your brain. They make you think you are seeing something that isn't really there. They can use color, light, or patterns **①** **to** do this. In order to understand what we see, first we get an image with our eye. The brain takes the picture from the eye. After that, it tries to understand the information. The picture in an optical illusion seems **②** **so real not as** reality. Naturally, the picture of reality is **③** **easier** to understand than that. That is why the brain thinks something is there that really isn't.

 ➔ _____

2. 다음 밑줄 친 부분을 바르게 고치세요.

● TOSEL 기출문제 변형 수능/내신 출제유형

2

White House is the place where the presidents of the United States of America live. There are many stories heard from the White House and one of them is about Abraham Lincoln's ghost. Abraham Lincoln is one of the **memorablest** presidents of United States of America. But after he died some people say that they saw Lincoln in White House. They said that Lincoln's ghost came knocking on their doors at night. Although this can be scary, people think of Lincoln's ghost as a protection and help in White House.

 _____

Answers

Short Answers

UNIT 1 p.23
▶ Activity
🖊 1. (a)   2. (b)   3. (b)   4. (a)   5. (c)   6. (b)   7. (a)   8. (c)   9. (a)   10. (b)

▶ Exercise 1 p.24
🖊 1. will, do   2. have   3. was   4. left   5. shows

▶ Exercise 2
🖊 1. is, rains   2. will attend   3. spent   4. will arrive   5. lives

▶ Exercise 3
1. invented   2. will play   3. wore   4. will clean   5. sleep

▶ Sentence Completion p.26
🖊 1. (B)   2. (C)   3. (A)   4. (B)   5. (C)   6. (B)   7. (A)   8. (C)   9. (B)   10. (B)

▶ Error Recognition p.28
🖊 1. (2) decide → decided   2. (5) tried → try

▶ Unit Review p.30
🖊 1. ❶ 현재의 상태   ❷ 습관인인 행위 동작   ❸ 불변의 진리·보편적 사실
   ❶ 현재의 상태 ➡ I am hungry now.   ❷ 습관인인 행위 동작 ➡ I take a shower every day.
   ❸ 불변의 진리·보편적 사실 ➡ The earth revolves around the sun.

🖊 2. ❶ 과거 한 시점에서의 동작·상태   ❹ 역사적 사실   ❺ 과거에서 본 미래
   ❶ 과거 한 시점에서의 동작·상태 ➡ I bought a leather wallet last weekend.
   ❷ 역사적 사실 ➡ The Korean War came to an end in 1953.
   ❸ 과거에서 본 미래 ➡ Anne said she would call me.

🖊 3. ❶ 단순미래   ❷ 의지미래
   ❶ 단순미래 ➡ The result will be successful.
   ❷ 의지미래 ➡ I will always support you.

UNIT 2 p.33
▶ Activity
🖊 1. (a)   2. (b)   3. (b)   4. (a)   5. (c)   6. (a)   7. (b)   8. (c)   9. (b)   10. (a)

▶ Exercise 1 p.34
🖊 1. is coming   2. gives   3. is doing   4. washes   5. is listening

▶ Exercise 2
1 was studying / called   2. called / was listening
3. was doing / came   4. met / were sightseeing
5. were chatting / cried

▶ Exercise 3
🖊 1. will be traveling   2. will be playing   3. will be washing   4. will be having   5. will be studying

▶ Sentence Completion p.36
🖊 1. (D)   2. (B)   3. (D)   4. (B)   5. (C)   6. (C)   7. (B)   8. (D)   9. (A)   10. (D)

▶ Error Recognition p.38
🖊 1. (1) play → playing   2. (2) touching → are touching

▶ Unit Review p.40
🖊 1. ❶ 현재 진행 중인 동작   ❹ 미래대용
   ❶ 현재 진행 중인 동작 ➡ She is drinking a cup of coffee.
   ❷ 미래대용 ➡ He is arriving at the train station tomorrow.
2. ❶ 과거 어느 시점의 진행 중인 동작   ❸ 과거 행위 중에 진행된 일
   ❶ 과거 어느 시점의 진행 중인 동작 ➡ I was writing an essay last night.
   ❷ 과거 행위 중에 진행된 일 ➡ They were playing soccer when I saw them.
3. ❶ 미래 한 시점에서의 동작의 진행
   ❶ 미래 한 시점에서의 동작의 진행 ➡ I will be making a speech here next Friday.

UNIT 3 p.43
▶ Activity
🖊 1. 계속   2. 경험   3. 결과   4. 완료   5. 계속   6. 완료   7. 경험   8. 완료   9. 계속   10. 결과

| ▶ Exercise 1 p.44 | 🖉 1. have studied | 2. have ever seen | 3. have already saved | 4. has written | 5. has watched |

| ▶ Exercise 2 | 🖉 1. has | 2. ago | 3. has grown | 4. so far | 5. before |

▶ Exercise 3

🖉 1. Have you ever seen her before?   2. He has studied abroad for five years.

3. How long have you been waiting for the train?

4. Today I read the newspaper while eating breakfast.   5. I haven't seen the new film yet.

▶ Sentence Completion p.46

🖉 1. (C) 2. (C) 3. (D) 4. (C) 5. (B) 6. (C) 7. (B) 8. (D) 9. (C) 10. (D)

▶ Error Recognition p.48

🖉 1. (1) has play → has played   2. (2) has have → has had

▶ Unit Review p.50

🖉 1. ❶ 완료   ❷ 경험   ❸ 계속   ❹ 결과

❶ 완료 ➡ They have already done their homework.

❷ 경험 ➡ We have never climbed the mountain.

❸ 계속 ➡ I have watched this movie for two hours.

❹ 결과 ➡ I have bought the pencil.

🖉 2. ❶ since   ❷ for   ❸ ago   ❹ before

❶ since ➡ I have had a headache since this morning.

❷ for ➡ I have had a headache for five hours.

❸ ago ➡ I called him one day ago.   ❹ before ➡ I have tried this food before.

UNIT 4 p.53

▶ Activity

🖉 1. (d) 2. (g) 3. (b) 4. (f) 5. (a) 6. (e) 7. (c)

| ▶ Exercise 1 p.54 | 🖉 1. as soon as | 2. before | 3. while | 4. until | 5. before |

| ▶ Exercise 2 | 🖉 1. When | 2. until | 3. while | 4. as | 5. Once |

| ▶ Exercise 3 | 🖉 1. since | 2. before | 3. when | 4. until | 5. As soon as |

▶ Sentence Completion p.56

🖉 1. (D) 2. (C) 3. (D) 4. (C) 5. (B) 6. (A) 7. (B) 8. (B) 9. (D) 10. (A)

▶ Error Recognition p.58

🖉 1. (3) when → while   2. (1) after → since

▶ Unit Review p.60

🖉 1. ❷ since   ❻ while   ❼ as

❽ till[until]   ❾ once   ❿ as soon as

🖉 ❶ since / I haven't watched a movie since I came here.

❷ while / I found my diary while I was cleaning my room.

❸ as / The baby opened her mouth as she said, "Mom."

❹ till[until] / The man sang in the park until it got dark.

❺ once / Once you hesitate, you lose good opportunities.

❻ as soon as / As soon as the class started, John entered the classroom.

🖉 ❶ when ❷ Since ❸ until ❹ while ❺ As ❻ before

TOSEL 실전문제 4

🖉 1. (A) 2. (D) 3. (C) 4. (B) 5. (A) 6. (B) 7. (D) 8. (C) 9. (D) 10. (A)

🖉 1. (1) will get → get   2. was → has been

UNIT 1 p.69

▶ Activity

🖉 1. 명사 2. 형용사 3. 부사 4. 명사 5. 부사 6. 명사 7. 명사 8. 형용사 9. 형용사 10. 부사

| ▶ Exercise 1 p.70 | 🖉 1. to do | 2. to be enjoying | 3. to escape | 4. to draw | 5. to find |

| ▶ Exercise 2 | 🖉 1. to play in | 2. to go out | 3. to get | 4. not to make | 5. to eat |

| ▶ Exercise 3 | 🖉 1. to become | 2. to donate | 3. to ask, to write | 4. to be | 5. not to fire |

▶ Sentence Completion p.72

🖉 1. (A) 2. (D) 3. (C) 4. (B) 5. (C) 6. (B) 7. (A) 8. (D) 9. (C) 10. (D)

▶ Error Recognition p.74

🖉 1. (5) be → to be   2. (3) to done → to do

✎ 1. ❶ to + 동사원형

   ❶ He is to meet his grandmother.   ❷ She became a teacher to teach young children.

✎ 2. ❶ 명사   ❷ 형용사   ❸ 부사

✎ ❶ 명사 ➡ I want to buy new shoes.   ❷ 형용사 ➡ I had no chance to talk about the issue.

   ❸ 부사 ➡ She is going abroad next month to study linguistics.

UNIT 2 p.79
▶ Activity

✎ 1. 주어 2. 보어 3. 목적어 4. 목적어 5. 주어 6. 목적어 7. 목적어 8. 주어 9. 보어 10. 목적어

▶ Exercise 1
p.80

✎ 1. departing   2. Traveling   3. baking   4. being   5. knitting

▶ Exercise 2

✎ 1. becoming   2. Building   3. seeing   4. finishing   5. answering

▶ Exercise 3

✎ 1. Playing basketball makes me feel happy.   2. x

   3. He enjoys drinking coffee every morning.   4. I suggested opening a new banking account to him.

   5. Grace looks forward to seeing her cousin.

▶ Sentence Completion
p.82

✎ 1. (C) 2. (B) 3. (C) 4. (A) 5. (B) 6. (B) 7. (C) 8. (A) 9. (C) 10. (C)

▶ Error Recognition
p.84

✎ 1. (5) learn - learning / to learn   2. (3) take - taking

▶ Unit Review
p.86

✎ 1. ❶ 동사원형 + -ing

   ❶ Her dog hates drinking water.   ❷ Traveling is my favorite hobby.

✎ 2. ❶ 주어   ❷ 목적어   ❸ 보어

   ❶ 주어 ➡ Learning is important to everyone.

   ❷ 목적어 ➡ I love jogging in the early morning.

   ❸ 보어 ➡ Her hobby is singing along with the K-pop singers.

UNIT 3 p.89
▶ Activity

✎ 1. (a) 2. (b) 3. (b) 4. (b) 5. (a) 6. (a) 7. (a) 8. (a) 9. (b) 10. (a)

▶ Exercise 1
p.90

✎ 1. talking   2. to make   3. to study, studying   4. eating   5. to buy

▶ Exercise 2

✎ 1. leaving   2. to learn   3. to correct   4. persuading   5. to exercise

▶ Exercise 3

✎ 1. to donate   2. having   3. going   4. to enroll   5. resigning

▶ Sentence Completion
p.92

✎ 1. (C) 2. (D) 3. (D) 4. (D) 5. (B) 6. (C) 7. (D) 8. (C) 9. (B) 10. (C)

▶ Error Recognition
p.94

✎ 1. (4) not buying - not to buy   2. (2) to take - taking

▶ Unit Review
p.96

✎ 1. ❶ 앞으로의 일   ❷ 지난 일

   ❶ 앞으로의 일 ➡ He remembers to meet them at the station.

   ❷ 지난 일 ➡ He remembers meeting them at the station.

   2. ❶ to부정사   ❷ 동명사

   ❶ to부정사 ➡ She expected her husband to remember their wedding anniversary.

   ❷ 동명사 ➡ He admitted violating the rules.

UNIT 4 p.99
▶ Activity

✎ 1. 내가 프로젝트를 끝낼 수 있도록 나를 도와준다니 그녀는 정말 착하다.

   2. 내가 창문을 닫아도 되니?   3. 그녀에게 그런 돈을 빌려주다니 그는 멍청하다.

   4. 나는 그녀가 이 곳에 오는 것이 좋다.   5. 그들은 내가 그 게임에 참여해야 한다고 주장했다.

   6. 나는 나의 손녀딸이 의사인 것이 자랑스럽다.   7. 내가 교수님을 뵈러 가는 것이 필요하다.

   8. 그들이 이 언어를 발명했다는 증거가 없다.   9. 그녀가 이 숙제를 끝내는 것은 어렵다.

   10. 나는 지하철이 너무 붐비는 것에 대해 불평했다.

▶ Exercise 1
p.100

✎ 1. for him   2. of her   3. for him   4. my   5. ø

▶ Exercise 2

✎ 1. for me   2. 생략   3. 맞는 문장   4. of you

▶ Exercise 3

✎ 1. his   2. her   3. for him   4. for him   5. of you

▶ Sentence Completion
p.102

✎ 1. (D) 2. (C) 3. (B) 4. (A) 5. (B) 6. (D) 7. (B) 8. (C) 9. (B) 10. (A)

▶ Error Recognition p.104	🖊	1. (4) The movie's → The movie		2. (2) of him → for him		

▶ Unit Review p.106	🖊	1. ❶ for + 목적격		❷ of + 목적격		

❶ for + 목적격 ➡ He ran slowly for his son to catch up with him.

❷ of + 목적격 ➡ It is clever of you to solve this difficult problem.

2. ❶ 소유격을 쓰는 경우　　　　❷ 소유격을 쓰지 않는 경우

❶ 소유격을 쓰는 경우 ➡ She is glad of her daughter's coming home.

❷ 소유격을 쓰지 않는 경우 ➡ The researcher is proud of his study showing a good result.

TOSEL 실전문제 5	🖊	1. (C)	2. (B)	3. (D)	4. (C)	5. (D)	6. (C)	7. (B)	8. (A)	9. (C)	10. (B)

🖊 1. (1) exploring → to explore　　　2. to play → playing 또는 play

CHAPTER 6　　　　　　　　　　　　　　　　　　　　　　　p.112

UNIT 1 p.115 ▶ Activity	🖊	1. more useful	2. the hottest	3. the easiest	4. more difficult	5. the most expensive
		6. closer	7. younger	8. the cheapest	9. warmer	10. the most comfortable

▶ Exercise 1 p.116	🖊	1. more complex	2. the most famous	3. the easiest	4. smaller	5. smarter

▶ Exercise 2	🖊	1. slower	2. more expensive	3. the prettiest	4. more difficult	5. faster

▶ Exercise 3	🖊	1. 맞는 문장	2. He was happier than me.

3. This room is the biggest room in this house.　4. That is the easiest way to go to school.

5. This new navigation is more useful than the old one.

▶ Sentence Completion p.118	🖊	1. (B)	2. (A)	3. (B)	4. (D)	5. (B)	6. (B)	7. (A)	8. (C)	9. (D)	10. (C)

▶ Error Recognition p.120	🖊	1. (1) the taller → the tallest		2. (5) more cheap → cheaper		

▶ Unit Review p.122	🖊	1. ❶ -e	❷ 자음 + y	❸ -ful, -ous, -ive 등으로 끝나는 2음절어

❶ -e / This puzzle is simpler than yours.

❷ 자음 + y / Speaking is easier than writing.

❸ -ful, -ous, -ive 등으로 끝나는 2음절어 / Jack is more famous than Dickson.

🖊 2. ❶ 자음 + y　　❷ -ful, -ous, -ive 등으로 끝나는 2음절어　　❸ 3음절어 이상

❶ 자음 + y / Speaking is the easiest of all activities.

❷ -ful, -ous, -ive 등으로 끝나는 2음절어 / Jack is the most famous person in the city.

❸ 3음절어 이상 / The white bag is the most expensive item in this store.

UNIT 2 p.125 ▶ Activity	🖊	1. better	2. most	3. last	4. less	5. upmost / uppermost
		6. least	7. worse	8. inmost / innermost	9. best	10. furthest

▶ Exercise 1 p.126	🖊	1. better	2. worst	3. farther	4. latest	5. less

▶ Exercise 2	🖊	1. less	2. latest	3. further	4. best	5. More

▶ Exercise 3	🖊	1. 맞는 문장	2. It was the least important part of this chapter.

3. I feel much better than yesterday thanks to the pill.

4. He arrived at the station later than had predicted.

5. His memory is worse than yours.

▶ Sentence Completion p.128	🖊	1. (B)	2. (A)	3. (B)	4. (D)	5. (B)	6. (C)	7. (D)	8. (C)	9. (B)	10. (C)

▶ Error Recognition p.130	🖊	1. (2) more good → better		2. (4) many → more		

▶ Unit Review p.132	🖊	1. ❶ worse	❷ latest(시간)	❸ last(순서)	❹ farther	❺ least

❶ worse / His memory is worse than yours.　❷ latest(시간) / I bought the latest smartphone.

❸ last(순서) / I checked the last email.　❹ farther / His house is farther from here than mine.

❺ least / The injuries are the least of her worries.

UNIT 3 p.135 ▶ Activity	🖊	1. 동등비교	2. 열등비교	3. 열등비교	4. 배수비교	5. 배수비교
		6. 배수비교	7. 배수비교	8. 열등비교	9. 동등비교	10. 배수비교

▶ Exercise 1 p.136	🖉	1. as fluently as	2. so smart as	3. so rich as	4. five times as thick as	5. as tall a student as

▶ Exercise 2	🖉	1. he	2. as expensive	3. so interesting	4. large	5. as many clothes

▶ Exercise 3	🖉	1. three times heavier than	2. five times as efficient as
		3. half as large as	4. two times the size
		5. not so polite as	

▶ Sentence Completion p.138

🖉 1. (A) 2. (C) 3. (A) 4. (A) 5. (A) 6. (A) 7. (C) 8. (A) 9. (D) 10. (B)

▶ Error Recognition p.140

🖉 1. (4) more beautiful → beautiful   2. (4) large → larger

▶ Unit Review p.142

🖉 1. ❶ as + 원급 + as

   ❶ as + 원급 + as ➡ Sue is as brave as John.

🖉 2. ❶ not as[so] + 원급 + as   ❷ less + 원급 + than

   ❶ not as[so] + 원급 + as ➡ Jane is not as[so] polite as Amy.

   ❷ less + 원급 + than ➡ Jane is less polite than Amy.

🖉 3. ❶ 배수사 + as + 원급 + as   ❷ 배수사 + the 명사 + of

   ❶ 배수사 + as + 원급 + as ➡ The ocean is three times as big as the lake.

   ❷ 배수사 + the 명사 + of ➡ The ocean is three times the size of the lake.

UNIT 4 p.145
▶ Activity

🖉 1. He is the tallest of all students. ➡ He is the tallest in his class.

2. This book is the most expensive of all books. ➡ This book is the most expensive in this shelf.

3. The baby is the cutest of all babies. ➡ The baby is the cutest in the kindergarten.

4. The statue is the highest of all artifacts. ➡ The statue is the highest in the world.

5. The Pacific is the widest of all oceans. ➡ The Pacific is the widest in the world.

▶ Exercise 1 p.146	🖉	1. the smartest	2. the cheapest	3. steepest	4. unhappiest	5. the richest

▶ Exercise 2	🖉	1. deepest	2. Most	3. greatest	4. hottest	5. fastest

▶ Exercise 3

🖉 1. This is the most expensive car you could ever find.

2. X

3. X

4. It was my biggest pleasure to go out with her.

5. Most of us participated in the survey.

▶ Sentence Completion p.148

🖉 1. (B) 2. (C) 3. (C) 4. (B) 5. (A) 6. (C) 7. (B) 8. (A) 9. (B) 10. (C)

▶ Error Recognition p.150

🖉 1. (1) the bigger → the biggest   2. (2) The most → Most

▶ Unit Review p.152

🖉 1. ❶ of all (the) + 복수명사[of + 복수대명사]   ❷ in (the) 장소   ❸ 명사 + (that)~ever[can]

   ❶ of all (the) + 복수명사[of + 복수대명사] ➡ This is the highest of all (the) buildings.

   ❷ in (the) 장소 ➡ This is the highest building in the world.

   ❸ 명사 + (that)~ever[can] ➡ This is the highest building (that) you could see.

🖉 2. ❷ 서술적으로 쓰인 최상급   ❺ '대부분의' 뜻일 때

   ❶ The mountain is highest at this point.

   ❷ 서술적으로 쓰인 최상급 ➡ Winter is coldest.

TOSEL 실전문제 6

🖉 1. (A) 2. (B) 3. (B) 4. (D) 5. (A) 6. (B) 7. (B) 8. (A) 9. (D) 10. (C)

🖉 1. (2) so real not as → not so real as   2. memorablest → most memorable

MEMO